STONEHENGE

& TIMBER CIRCLES

Alex Gibson

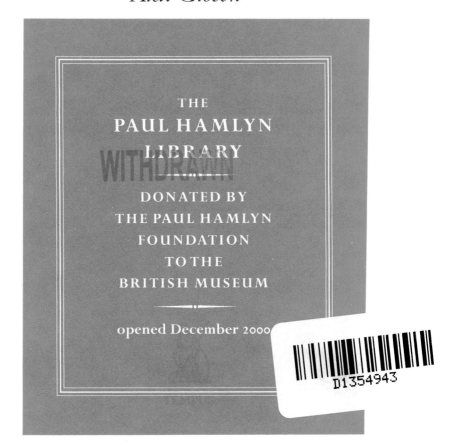

First published 1998
First paperback edition 2000

PUBLISHED IN THE UNITED KINGDOM BY:

Tempus Publishing Ltd
The Mill, Brimscombe Port
Stroud, Gloucestershire GL5 2QG

PUBLISHED IN THE UNITED STATES OF AMERICA BY:

Tempus Publishing Inc.
2A Cumberland Street
Charleston, SC 29401

Tempus books are available in France, Germany and Belgium
from the following addresses:

Tempus Publishing Group	Tempus Publishing Group	Tempus Publishing Group
21 Avenue de la République	Gustav-Adolf-Straße 3	Place de L'Alma 4/5
37300 Joué-lès-Tours	99084 Erfurt	1200 Brussels
FRANCE	GERMANY	BELGIUM

British Library Cataloguing in Publication Data.
A catalogue record for this book is available from the British Library.

ISBN 0 7524 1492 5

Typesetting and origination by Tempus Publishing.
PRINTED AND BOUND IN GREAT BRITAIN.

Contents

The illustrations

Text figures

Colour plates (between pages 64 and 65)

Introduction

Timber circles have, until comparatively recently, been a largely ignored group of monuments. This is because, unlike their stone counterparts, little survives above ground to suggest the complexity which must, at one time, have existed. It is a case of out of sight, out of mind. Timber circles, because they do not survive as standing monuments, are also the subject of conjectural reconstructions. Some of these are considered and plausible. Others are less so but, because of the ambiguity of the evidence, are difficult to challenge. Reconstruction is largely a case of personal preference. This conjecture, and all that it implies, does little to enamour the sometimes too level-headed archaeologist. However, to the present writer, it is the unknown, indeed perhaps the unknowable, which harbours the fascination of these sites.

Despite their attempts at invisibility, there is a surprising number of timber circles as a glance at the corpus will indicate. This is not a finite number and others will doubtless come to light through increased aerial photography and accidental excavation; for example, the excavation of composite monuments or the excavation of gravel terraces where pre-evaluation geophysical survey has failed to detect the pits of the circle amongst its naturally pitted background. Aerial photography has been foremost in detecting these elusive sites though it must be remembered that aerial photographs show circles of pits, not all of which necessarily need have held posts **(fig 1)**. The corpus is, therefore, a growing one — one which will expand as archaeological investigation develops.

This book attempts to unravel some of the secrets of these enigmatic sites. It cannot hope to unravel them all. Nor can it hope to apply blanket explanations to a site type which is distributed widely over Britain and Ireland and which has a currency of over two millennia in the archaeological record. During this considerable period and over such an area it might be expected that functions changed emphasis and rituals differed in their directions. Nevertheless by looking closely at these sites, at their associations, their layouts and their contexts, some reconstructions of past ceremonies and uses can be attempted. Some insights into the beliefs and practices of the builders can be gained. However it is hoped that fact rather than fantasy will guide the analysis.

All the radiocarbon dates quoted in this text are either in their laboratory form (ie BP) or are in calibrated years BC. The 1986 curve has been used in all calibrations. Bibliographical references are given in the Harvard form but no textual reference is given to the excavation reports of timber circles; these may be found in the catalogue. Comprehensive plans of timber circles may be found in an earlier paper (Gibson 1994).

1   *Insall's photograph of Woodhenge taken in 1925 which discovered the internal series of pits.*

Acknowledgements

Other than to the sources of the photographs and illustrations which are acknowledged in the captions, the writer is indebted to Dr A Burl who commented on earlier drafts of the text. Information in advance of publication has been supplied by Helmut Becker, Martin Green, Jan de Jong, Graham Ritchie, Helen Roche and Percival Turnbull. Thanks lastly but importantly go to my former employers, the Clwyd-Powys Archaeological Trust, who kindly appointed me director of the Sarn-y-bryn-caled excavations, the site which kindled my interest in timber circles. Little did we know quite how it would turn out.

1 Britain at the time of timber circles

Unlike other relatively short-lived monument types such as long barrows or causewayed enclosures, the currency of timber circles spans a considerable period. Present evidence suggests that they appear in the archaeological record at about 3000 BC and decline in importance almost two thousand years later. This is a substantial time-slice involving two millennia of human development. To modern minds, time tends to lose its significance with increasing remoteness; thus terms such as 'Neolithic' command little more consideration than might the similar term 'Edwardian'. Yet this is despite the fact that the Neolithic occupied more centuries than the Edwardian period did decades. The two millennia in which timber circles were built and used in Britain represents a period between the present day and the age of Rome; from gladiators and chariots to space travel.

The period can also be expanded and extended to the first century BC if one considers the later Irish evidence. But while these later circles will be considered in subsequent chapters, on current knowledge they lie well beyond the main period of currency of this class of Neolithic and Bronze Age monument. The Irish material appears, rather, to mark a re-emergence of the timber circle tradition, perhaps a monumental phenomenon preserved in the oral record, in legends of by-gone days when ancestors and their deeds were remembered and doubtless glorified. By including the Irish sites it can be effectively demonstrated that timber circles span the prehistory of these islands from the establishment of agriculture to the advance of Rome. If we look to Europe, then the time-span can be extended still further, for example back to the fifth millennium BC in Bavaria.

The time-span analogy is not altogether realistic. While it serves to demonstrate the longevity of the prehistoric period, it is also acknowledged that cultures often develop at an increased rate as their technology develops and it is generally accepted that our own development has been rapidly accelerating since the invention of the steam engine and, more recently, the transistor and the microchip. But nevertheless, a friend who has traced his family tree back to sixteenth-century Amsterdam (1580s), has documented thirteen generations in these 400 years. Translate this into great, great-great and great-great-great grandparents then multiply it by five to cover 2000 years and one comprehends the time-scale involved and, perhaps, the importance of ancestry to more technologically primitive societies.

For a millennium prior to 3000 BC agriculture had been practised in Britain and Ireland. This economic regime, the first agricultural revolution, reached these shores from

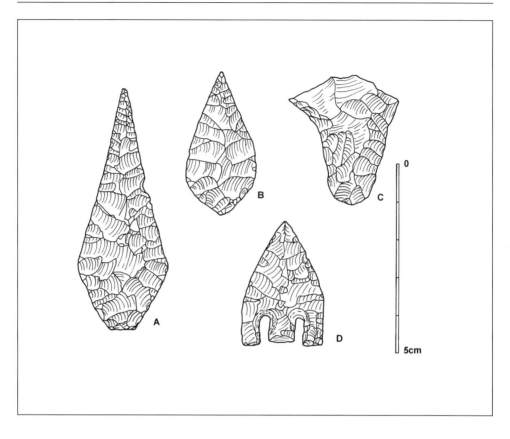

2   Various arrowhead types. A-C from Yorkshire (after Kinnes), D from mid-Wales.

continental Europe though the mechanics of its spread, whether by invasion, adoption or, more likely, an uneven combination of both, are still not fully understood. It is likely that both elements played a part. For example seed corn and domesticated animals such as pigs, sheep/goats (it is difficult to distinguish skeletally between primitive sheep and goats) and cattle would have required transporting across the channel by people, but then this new economic basis was subsequently adopted by the native Mesolithic hunter-gatherers. With this new, largely sedentary lifestyle came the knowledge of pottery which is one of the most closely datable artefacts of Prehistory and which is a vital tool for prehistorians who try to reconstruct a relative prehistoric time-scale, who try to identify cultural and regional groupings within prehistoric societies, and who try to define economic relationships between different geographical areas. This distinctive artefact will be discussed again below.

To return to agriculture, the introduction of farming had a marked effect on the local environment and landscape. Large areas of forest were felled with the aid of stone axes and grazing herds, the ground was tilled and planted, the harvest reaped, animals fed and slaughtered. Grazing animals continued to help keep the forest at bay. Wild resources were also exploited. The bones of ferile animals, for example red deer, in faunal assemblages

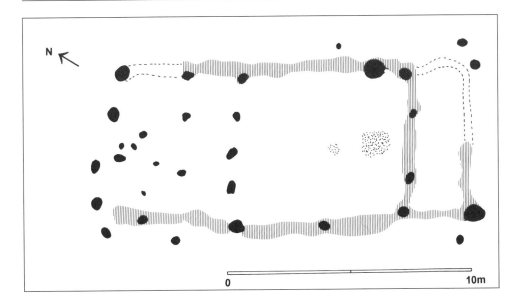

3   *The Ballyglass house of posthole and bedding trench construction. The stippled areas are hearths (after Grogan).*

and the presence of wild fruit seeds and hazelnuts on many Neolithic sites attest that the hunter-gatherer ways were not altogether forgotten. While Mesolithic populations were doubtless aware of the cyclical nature of the seasons and the cycles of the faunal and floral resources on which they were dependent, Neolithic farmers were probably even more aware of the cycles of the sun and seasons. There would have been specific periods of time for planting and reaping — times which, if ignored or missed, could lead to starvation and thus threaten the society's very existence.

Mother Earth also provided, as she still does, the materials for the manufacture of tools **(fig 2)**. Stone for axes and corn-grinding querns, flint for knives, arrowheads and tools for scraping hides, and clay for pottery. Clay, dug from riverbanks, was mixed and fashioned into a variety of forms, fired in bonfires and used for the cooking and storing of meats as well as ending up in religious contexts. Pottery, bulky, heavy and comparatively fragile, was more suited to a sedentary group than a mobile one and it is only with the Neolithic that pottery is found in these islands.

The houses of the first farmers tend to be rectangular **(fig 3)** and of sufficient size to accommodate a family group (see Darvill 1996 for a corpus, though some of the floor plans are subjective). Their survival is rare however, and little with certainty can be said of these early peoples' social structure from their settlements alone **(colour plate 1)**. However, large communal monuments were also constructed and appear to have had a clear mortuary role. Long barrows and chambered tombs were elongated mounds with timber or stone chambers which housed the mortal remains of often numerous individuals **(fig 4)**; or rather parts of numerous individuals since complete skeletons are rarely encountered. There seems to have been a practice of excarnation prior to the burial

4   *Facade of the long cairn at Cairnholy.*

of the skeletal remains. These large mounds, often with long flanking quarry ditches, certainly appear to be communal constructions and may well lie at territorial boundaries (Kinnes 1992).

Also communal in their effort are the causewayed enclosures (see Mercer 1990 for a useful introduction). These large banked and ditched enclosures, quarried from the chalks and gravels with antler picks and bone scoops or shovels, are characterised by ditches which are broken into numerous short segments. They appear to have been seasonal fairs or meeting places and the remains of feasts have been found there. But they also had both domestic and mortuary roles. Hembury in Devon, Hambledon Hill in Hampshire and Crickley Hill in Gloucester were all the scenes of attacks and numerous arrowheads have been found at these sites. Also at Hambledon Hill and Windmill Hill in Wiltshire human remains occur in the ditches, including the burials of infants. At Hambledon Hill, partially articulated human remains were found suggesting the exposure of corpses and, on the floors of the ditches, deliberately placed skulls were found, some with cervical vertebrae still attached **(fig 5)**.

In the few centuries either side of 3000 BC, the dawn of timber circles, there appears to have been a change in the old ways. There is evidence for scrub regeneration in some areas of, for example, the Wessex chalklands, and causewayed enclosures and long barrows, while still on occasion visited, appear to be abandoned in favour of more diverse burial customs and more formalised enclosures. The ceramics develop into heavy, thick-walled and highly decorated vessels named Peterborough Ware **(fig 6)** after the site where the pottery style was first recognised. Peterborough and related wares elsewhere in Britain and Ireland comprise round based bowls adorned with impressed decoration; that is

5   *Human skull on the*
     floor of the main
     causewayed enclosure
     ditch at Hambledon
     Hill
     (Courtesy of Roger
     Mercer).

decoration made by impressing objects such as the articulated ends of the bones of birds and small mammals, twigs or string into the wet clay to form a variety of motifs and designs (Gibson & Woods 1997). Peterborough Ware has been recognised as a facet of a larger, more widespread impressed ware tradition which has a pan-British and Irish distribution. The rims of these vessels are thick and heavy and they too are decorated but the decoration usually stops towards the lower third of the pots suggesting that this area was not visible, and therefore there was no point in decorating it. This is a logical assumption. The pots with their generally rounded bases could not stand except in rounded hollows in beaten earth floors or with the aid of a stabilising device such as a rope quoit. Equally they were well-designed for cooking in open fires, the rounded bases sitting well in glowing embers. Either way, the lower third could not be seen. Carbonised remains on some vessels do indeed indicate that these pots were used for cooking and

6   Highly decorated Peterborough Ware from Sarn-y-bryn-caled, Powys (© CPAT).

scientific analysis of the residues absorbed by and preserved within the fabric of Peterborough vessels in mid-Wales has demonstrated that they contained the fats of ruminant animals such as sheep and cattle.

However, there was more to making ceramics than simply creating vessels in which to cook. The decoration, as already mentioned, was often elaborate and the restricted nature of the decorative motifs and techniques employed suggest a long-forgotten symbolism apparently alien to modern society. There is also a current theory that the inclusions within the fabric of the pots had more than a utilitarian purpose. This requires a short explanation. When fired in a bonfire in which temperatures can often rise rapidly and then fluctuate, the water in clay can quickly boil and convert to steam. This steam expands and finds a way to escape from its clay matrix. If escape routes are blocked, the steam can explode through the fabric of the pot which unfortunately results in chunks of pottery being blown out of the vessel walls. The fired pots will be broken and incomplete. To facilitate the escape of this steam, non-clay particles were added to the mix and these provided capillaries between the clay and the inclusions through which the steam could pass and thus the vessels could survive the firing intact (Gibson & Woods 1997). Almost anything could be mixed with clay to produce this safety valve, but there is a growing amount of evidence to suggest that there were deliberate selections being exercised. Quartz is a favourite. In other ceramics burnt flint, despite its razor sharp edges, was also chosen. Grog, pieces of crushed up pottery, seems to be the most practical of the choices made. Were these materials chosen for more than simply utilitarian purposes? The evidence is not conclusive and work is in progress, but there do seem to be some deliberate selections being made. In the case of quartz, for example, its presence on ritual sites is well known and the rock itself may have had a mythological significance. Thus the production of pottery may have ritual interwoven in its fabric.

Peterborough Ware dates to around 3000 BC. Settlements associated with this ceramic are rare even allowing for the fact that the distinction between religious and secular is not easily drawn in Prehistory. The main evidence for domestic activity comes from pits and postholes with little structural evidence to suggest the house types inhabited by these people. Pits are variously interpreted as storage pits, rubbish pits or ritual depositories. The first two interpretations are related for it seems from Iron Age contexts that pits used for the storage of grain and foodstuffs became, when contaminated and soured by over use, convenient 'land-fill' sites for the deposition of rubbish. There is yet another link for some of these rubbish pits appear to have had ritually charged and deliberately placed material in their initial deposits. In fact the evidence for Neolithic storage pits is scarce. The majority of pits from this period are shallow and while some may have lost portions of their upper levels to modern agriculture, others, where protected for example by barrow mounds, appear always to have been shallow **(colour plate 2)**. The rubbish pit theory is also not without problems. Why bother to bury rubbish? Why not just throw it on the fields or stockpile it in middens, especially where the material does not present a health hazard (eg pottery and flint)? Recent analysis of material from mid-Wales indicates that the flint had been trampled prior to its deposition, and rarely are complete pots present in these pits. Do we have deliberate selection here? Do these pits have a ritual function? The term 'structured deposition' is becoming increasingly used in Neolithic contexts but really does little to further our interpretation of the data. Structured deposition means that the material is deliberately placed. It does not tell us why. The data therefore are open to various interpretations.

House sites are also open to interpretation and reinterpretation. At Cefn Bryn on the Gower peninsula, for example, a bedding trench and a hearth associated with fine Peterborough Vessels were interpreted as the remains of a dwelling. At Cefn Cilsanws in southern Powys a small oval stake-built structure was also interpreted as a dwelling and Peterborough Ware was found nearby **(fig 7)**. An apparent rectangular wall and post-built structure was located beneath a cairn at Mount Pleasant in Mid Glamorgan. These sites were all from protected contexts which account for the preservation of such flimsy evidence.

Evidence for the burial practices of the users of Peterborough Ware is as flimsy as the houses. A cremation was found in a pit with Peterborough Ware at Whitton Hill in Northumberland. At the rock-shelter of Church Dale in Derbyshire, a Mortlake style bowl was found with a contracted inhumation. Both these finds suggest a preference towards the burials of individuals as opposed to the multiple deposits frequently, though not universally, encountered in the earlier Neolithic.

Sometime before 2700 BC, a new pottery style enters the archaeological stage. This ceramic is characterised by tub, barrel or bucket-shaped vessels with flat bases and often highly decorated surfaces adorned with geometric incised motifs as well as cordons either stuck onto the outside or raised from the vessel wall. This is called Grooved Ware and marks the style of pottery most commonly associated with the large Wessex henges and the more complex timber circles **(fig 8)**.

Like Peterborough Ware, Grooved Ware is widely distributed over the UK and Ireland.

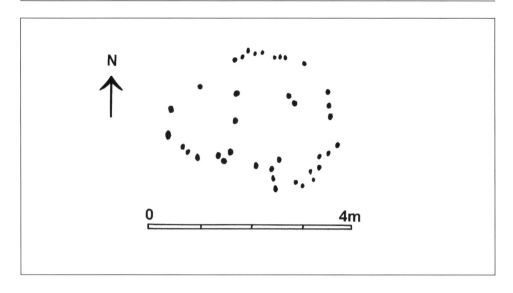

7   *Plan of the possible Peterborough Ware house at Cefn Cilsanws, Powys (after Webley).*

Once more pit sites and house sites are associated with this ceramic but rarely burials, at least not directly. Grooved Ware is also associated with a distinct artefact range, often artefacts of considerable quality and workmanship — maceheads of antler and flint, highly polished knives, chisel-edged arrowheads and elaborate bone pins. Many of these artefacts, by virtue of their exotic nature or conspicuous consumption of manpower, have been labelled prestige goods or 'symbols of power'. The elaborately carved and polished flint macehead from Knowth in County Meath is arguably one of the finest examples of the skill of the Neolithic artesan with perfect spirals being engraved into solid flint and the macehead perforated by a near-perfect cylindrical hole **(fig 9)**.

It was stated above that Grooved Ware pots are not directly associated with burial. This is not strictly true. They are not associated in the same way as some of the Peterborough and later pots where a specific vessel will accompany a specific burial. Instead, multiple Grooved Ware vessels might accompany collected burials in passage-tombs or be loosely associated with burials which are occasionally found in henge ditches. Human remains may also occur on timber circles with which Grooved Ware is a common find.

On the large ritual sites of Wessex, Grooved Ware occurs in substantial quantities. In particular henges which are circular or oval enclosures with external banks and internal ditches, an arrangement which does not suggest a defensive function (Burl 1991). At the henge of Durrington Walls it was found in the ditch, the postholes of the timber circle and in a midden deposit. At Woodhenge the Grooved Ware was both in the ditch and also below the bank, suggesting a phase of use prior to the construction of the henge and possibly associated with the earlier timber circle. The nature of the ceramics from these sites has often been discussed. Is it ritual? Is it domestic? In fact the answer can be both. The carbonaceous products on some vessel walls indicate that they had been used for cooking, but the ultimate deposition of the pots also argues in favour of a ritual use, albeit

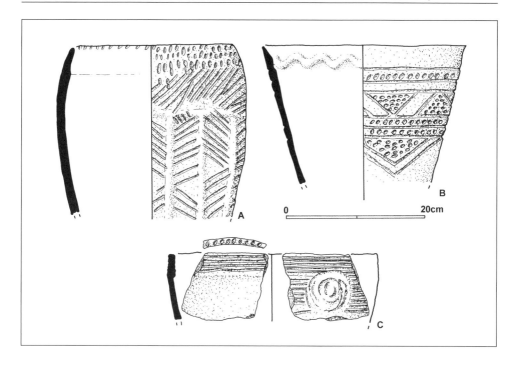

8   *Grooved Ware. A & C from Durrington Walls, B from Clacton (after Longworth).*

9   *Drawing of the Knowth flint macehead, expanded to show all the decoration (after O'Sullivan).*

17

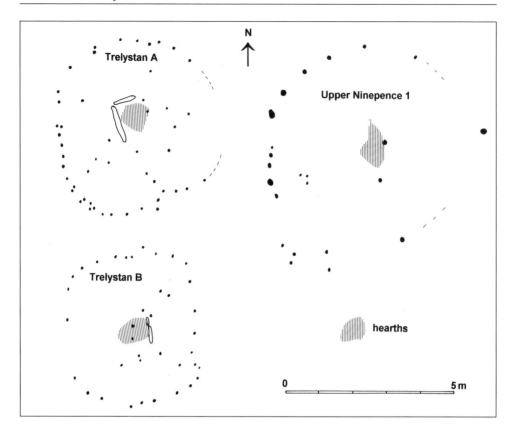

10   *The Grooved Ware house plans from Trelystan and Walton, Powys (Trelystan after Britnell).*

probably ultimately. This is not contradictory. In many religions, the mundane can often be elevated to a position of great religious significance. Thus eggs at Easter symbolise new life and regeneration while candles at Christmas herald advent.

As well as these religious contexts, Grooved Ware is also found on sites whose interpretation is likely to be domestic. At Walton in Powys, for example, a roughly circular stake-walled structure some 5m in diameter was discovered and associated with the Grooved Ware phase of the site. This had an entrance to the south-west and surrounded a central hearth. Two similar structures were found at Trelystan near Welshpool, also in Powys **(fig 10)**. Sealed beneath barrows, these flimsy structures were likewise demarcated by stakehole walls and defined an area some 4m square. Internally, a central rectangular hearth was edged with stones and pits containing heat-cracked stones probably suggest cooking. These small modest sites contrast strikingly with the large timber circles with which Grooved Ware is synonymous. But they serve to indicate the range of sites with which this often highly decorated ceramic is associated. They also strengthen the case for the multi-purpose interpretation with, perhaps, domestic vessels ultimately achieving ritual deposition.

In the couple of centuries prior to 2000BC, there is a distinct horizon in the British and

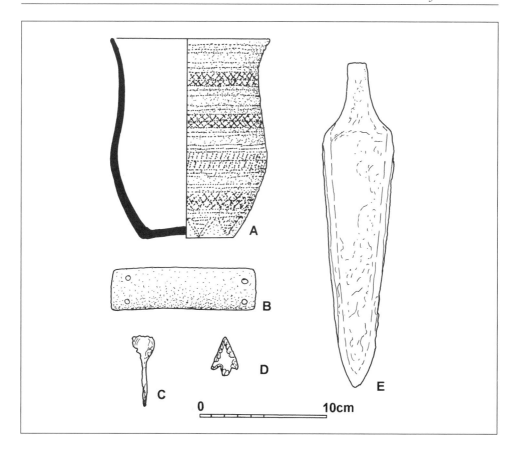

11   The Beaker grave group from Roundway G8, Wiltshire. A — Beaker, B — wristguard, C— copper awl, D — barbed and tanged arrowhead, E — dagger (after Case).

Irish archaeological records marked by the arrival, from the Continent, of a distinctive pottery type known as the Beaker or Bell Beaker and an associated artefact package **(fig 11)** (Case 1995). Distinctive tool types with which this pottery is found include small flint scrapers called button or thumbnail scrapers, V-perforated jet buttons, peculiar perforated and polished stone bars usually called archers' wristguards (though their real function is unknown), barbed and tanged flint arrowheads and the appearance of the first metals in the form of copper and gold trinkets soon followed by copper and bronze artefacts such as axes and daggers. The users of Beakers are also, wrongly, accredited with the introduction of the rite of individual burial.

So striking is this artefact package, and so uniform its distribution over Europe, that it was generally believed that the appearance of the pots in Britain represented an invasion by archer warriors who buried their dead in the foetal or crouched position in single graves beneath round barrows. Analysis of the archaeological data, however, demonstrates that crouched burial had been practised among the diverse burial practices of earlier periods and that no monument types or economic differences were introduced by the supposed invaders, who, instead, seemed to assimilate immediately within the existing archaeological background. Consequently the idea of an invasion was abandoned in favour of a cult package being adopted by the indigenous peoples. Clearly there would have had to have been European contact since the pots do not themselves move, but this contact may have been through trade and exchange rather than aggressive incursion.

Certainly Beaker pots, distinctive elegant fine-walled vessels, are found in contexts most similar to the Grooved Ware and Peterborough vessels described above. Except that Beakers are found in graves much more commonly than are the earlier types. Henges, timber circles, long barrow and causewayed enclosure ditches, house sites and middens all yield Beaker sherds in varying quantities; occasionally considerable quantities. Some 10,000 sherds are, for example, reported to have been found at the coastal sand dune site at Northton on the Isle of Harris (Simpson 1976).

At this site, nestling in silver sands below the rocky height of Toe Head and overlooking the Isle of Ensay across a narrow stretch of often turquoise sea, the remains of two buildings were found. The better preserved was sunk slightly into the sand and revetted with upright stones. It was oval in plan, open to the wider south-west end and contained an internal pit and hearth **(fig 12)**. Small stakeholes between the outer wall and the central area probably represent some internal arrangements or perhaps, though less likely, roof supports. The structure, measuring just under 9m long by about 4m wide, was large enough to accommodate a family group and this is the pattern for the majority of British domestic structures found to date from this period.

In addition to their distinctive potting technology, their artefact package and their distinctive individual burials, Beakers also coincide with the appearance of metalwork. At first gold and copper trinkets appear: sun discs and button caps as well as peculiar rolled sheets of decorated gold, usually called basket earrings but more likely to be hair rings. These elaborate objects are clearly decorative rather than functional and must have been used for display and personal adornment. The sun discs, appearing rather like gold milk-bottle tops, have geometric decoration, usually a cross, embossed onto the surface. Small holes or nicks in the edges indicate that they were originally stitched onto a fabric or some other organic backing. Variations of the design are conical rather than flat and were used to cover conical jet or bone buttons. The earrings, where found in graves, are normally found at the side of the head of the skeleton and hence their interpretation. However, if such they were, the 'basket' side would have hung downwards and the decoration would have been largely hidden. If they were worn down the side of the face, from the temple to the jaw, wrapped around hair in much the same way as some present-day Jewish sects have ringlets or as native Americans are frequently portrayed, then both camps are satisfied. They would still be found at the side of the skeleton's head and the decoration would also be visible.

With the appearance of gold comes also the introduction of copper and later the addition of tin and later still arsenic to make bronze. The two metals are of course *superficially* related and this may be in part responsible for their simultaneous appearance in the archaeological record. For example, both metals are relatively easy to work, they both gleam and they are both found in a natural state, though prospecting for ores became increasingly common as the demand grew. The superficial visual similarity of the two

12   The Beaker House at Northton, Harris (Courtesy of Derek Simpson).

metals, gold and bronze, is also something which is rarely remembered. In graves and similar contexts, we are used to finding corroded green copper and bronze artefacts stained by the ravages of time. But, when new, these copper-alloy daggers and axes would have gleamed in the sun, perhaps giving rise to the later mythical use of golden (bronze?) sickles by the Celtic priesthood. This is not to suggest that, like modern-day tourists in a bazaar, the early prehistoric metal-users were confused by these different materials, nor that they could not tell the difference, but is rather intended to draw an oft-forgotten similarity between the visual properties of the two metals.

As the new medium gained popularity and became used more widely for weaponry and tools, so the raw material was traded. Existing trade networks were doubtless used and it is interesting to note that copper was traded in a form already recognisable and indeed familiar within these networks: the axe. Copper and copper-alloy flat axes and moulds are common finds (Cowie 1988) and, like their stone precursors, some were used while others appear to have been buried in pristine condition or even an unfinished, unsharpened state. This phenomenon is yet more proof that the underlying structure of society remained. It may not have remained unaltered, but the basic fabric still remained.

Beaker pots left their influence on the earlier Bronze Age ceramics. In Ireland in particular, vase-shaped pots with geometric decoration are probably local equivalents of late Beaker. In Scotland too, particularly on the fringes, vase-shaped vessels appear to be local Beaker imitations, particularly in the Stone Houses of Shetland and the settlements of the Western Isles. But the underlying native traditions re-emerge in an altered and

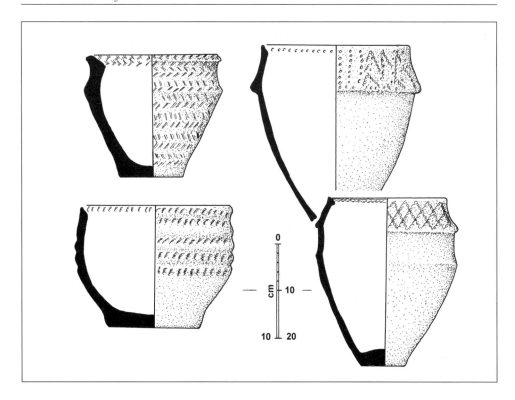

13   *Food Vessels and Collared Urns. Top left, vase food vessel from Northumberland. Bottom left, bowl food vessel from Lanarkshire (after Simpson). Top right, bipartite Collared Urn from Cleveland (after Longworth). Bottom right, tripartite Collared Urn from Strathclyde (after Longworth).*

developed state in the form of Food Vessels and Collared Urns **(fig 13)**. These too are frequently found in graves, usually individual burials either by cremation or inhumation. The term 'Food Vessel' was given to this often squat and thick-walled ceramic because the early antiquaries wished to distinguish it from the thin-walled Beaker. Beakers, as the name suggests, were considered to be drinking cups while the thick heavy rims of the later vessels made them unsuitable cups. Thus they were assumed to hold food. While this unproven assumption would not be entertained today, nevertheless the name has become embedded in the archaeological terminology and is now used to describe the vessel type rather than its function. Collared Urns are recognised by their heavy rims on top of a tapering body. They often reach substantial sizes, in excess of 50cm high. This time, as the name suggests, these pots were used to contain the cremated bones of the deceased. They were normally inverted over the cremation.

Within the monument tradition, round barrows and cairns were still the primary funerary monument. They often covered a primary and several secondary burials. These too often reach substantial sizes, particularly when on crest or sky-line positions and may, like the long barrows before them, have served a territorial as well as funerary purpose **(fig**

14   Copt Hill round barrow, Tyne and Wear.

14). Other sites are more modest but may well be clustered into cemeteries. Some of the most impressive of these are to be found in Wessex but the visually impressive aerial photographs of clustered ring-ditches, the remains of ploughed-out barrows, on the gravel terraces of nearly all our river valleys indicate that the phenomenon was widespread.

Henges continue into the Bronze Age **(fig 15)** but become smaller and more varied in their internal arrangements. At the smaller end of the spectrum, they blend into the numerous other circular sepulchro-ritual monuments: ring-ditches, ring cairns, enclosed cremation cemeteries and penannular ring-ditches. Existing henges take on a sepulchral role with Food Vessel burials in, for example, Balfarg, Milfield North and North Mains.

There is, however, another change at this period. Despite the continuation of the established monuments, there appears to be a move towards openness in religion, towards accessibility to the rites and ceremonies practised. It will be seen in subsequent chapters that at henges and timber circles, including Stonehenge, its stones shaped by woodworkers, there is evidence to suggest a distinct attempt to exclude certain members of the population from parts of the monuments. For example, the banks of henges, exaggerated at the entrances to restrict vision into the interior, the placing of the bluestones within the sarsen circle at Stonehenge denying sightlines into the horseshoes, the planked walls at timber circles with their often channelled entrances — all serve to deny visual if not physical access to the interior of these monuments. This changes with stone circles.

Spanning the later Neolithic and earlier Bronze Age, and frequently replacing timber circles, these megalithic rings can impressively define an area, can enclose the orchestra on which the ceremonies are played and can separate the sacred from the profane. They

15   *Aerial photograph of the Dyffryn Lane henge complex, Powys (photo Chris Musson,*
      © CPAT).

cannot, however, hide the rituals from spectators. At some sites the stones are widely spaced, almost encouraging viewers **(colour plate 3)**, at others the stones were so small as to have offered no obstacle to the hungry onlookers — assuming, of course, that there were some. At the end of the stone circle sequence, small settings of four stones — four-posters — provide rarely enough internal room for little more than a burial (Burl 1976). Times, and with them practices, had changed.

Stone circles, with standing stones and stone rows, form some of the most enduring classes of monument to survive from this period **(fig 16)**. They are emotive and are more or less unique in that they can be viewed today much as they would have been viewed by their users, if not their builders. As such, they preserve evidence for use and beliefs which timber circles, by view of their medium, have lost. Thus lunar and solar observation can be demonstrated at some sites, height variation in stones can be seen at others, and internal arrangements can be discerned within still more. Where orientations in circles can be demonstrated, there is enough evidence now to indicate the observance of the moon and solar orb at distinct times of the year, times which later become known as the major Celtic festivals — midsummer, midwinter, spring and harvest. These were all times of the year important to farming communities when doubtless rituals and celebrations took place in order to ensure the continuity of Mother Earth's providence and preserve the order of society.

The link between stone and timber circles is at times contradictory. Common orientations can sometimes be demonstrated at both types of sites. They are both circular.

16   The Fourstones stone circle, Walton, Powys.

They are both on occasion found within henges. They both decrease in size through time and take on a more sepulchral role. They both share common alignments. But there appears to be a fundamental difference: a change of emphasis from the restricted to the available, from the hidden to the accessible.

This is particularly demonstrable at some of the larger multiple sites, where, even if not screened, vision to the interior of the timber circle would have been restricted by virtue of the density of the posts. These sites are often replaced by stone circles at, for example, Balfarg, the Sanctuary and, more recently (if presumably), Stanton Drew.

Settlements in the early Bronze Age take on much the same pattern as those in the preceding periods. A sand dune site at Ardnave on Islay, for example, was very similar in general form to that at Northton; a slightly sunken oval structure with stone revetment and associated with a large quantity of Food Vessel pottery. Further south, in Northumberland, an early Bronze Age settlement at Houseledge comprised round timber houses set on platforms terraced into the hillside and which were associated with field systems and Cordoned Urn pottery. In Wales, at Glanfeinion, a timber round house was excavated on the river terrace of the Severn, also associated with Cordoned Urn pottery and radiocarbon dates of around 1400-1200 BC (Britnell *et al.* 1997). In southern Britain, round timber houses also seem to prevail. These too are often terraced into the hillside and, like sites such as Itford Hill, may be clustered and associated with field systems. On Dartmoor, the whole of the fringes of the moor seem to have been enclosed in a single act dividing the landscape into territories around a common upland grazing area **(fig 17)**. This work and the human resources involved clearly points to a highly organised and structured society.

This brief chronological survey spans approximately two millennia of human

17   Prehistoric rectangular fields near Kestor, Dartmoor.

development in Britain: the period which saw the decline and fall of the timber circle tradition. Such a brief resumé cannot do justice to the complexities of some individual issues of the time but it is hoped that it serves as a backcloth on which to superimpose some of the events documented in forthcoming chapters. Above all it must be remembered that it is people who are responsible for the archaeological record. The artefacts they left behind were created by people for people. All things had meaning and purpose, society was structured and lifecycles had to be maintained. Religion or belief systems are endemic to agricultural societies who depend on the Earth for subsistence and the sun for life. Both would require constant appeasement to ensure their goodwill. Timber circles are just one facet of how these duties were fulfilled.

2 The context of timber circles

Between 3000 and 1000 BC, timber circles occupy a number of different monumental contexts. Being sites which are widely distributed in both time and space, it is logical to assume that the rituals practised within these sites may have changed or developed over these two millennia. The details of the rituals practised may also have differed geographically and there may have been significant differences in the ceremonies taking place at, for example, North Mains in Perthshire and Durrington Walls, almost 400 miles (640km) to the south in Wiltshire, far less the Continental European sites. However, the architectural similarities and the orientations within many sites suggest that the circles within this time period must be related to each other within a general common ritual/religious tradition. For example, at Stonehenge and other timber circle sites, there is evidence for the observance of solar and lunar positions at different times of the year. Solar and lunar observation was a practice which continued well into the Christian period and major midsummer, midwinter, vernal and autumnal festivals, their actual timing determined by the positions of the sun and the moon, are common to the majority of contemporary, and therefore probably past, religions. If this is accepted, then it stands to reason that some sites may share aspects of common monumental patterning in, for example, their relationship with other monument forms.

Timber circles are either freestanding or form a component of another monument. In the latter case, they usually represent a primary component in those instances where they occupy a particular phase in a larger monument's history and rarely are they added to an existing monument. They also occur on their own or within a ritual complex.

Free-standing sites are perhaps the easiest to consider first. Sarn-y-bryn-caled is one example where the timber circle stands unassociated with any other monumental component even though it does form part of a ritual complex **(fig 18)**. This site has no surrounding bank or ditch, it does not, as far as excavation could demonstrate, lie within a sacred enclosure nor was it later covered by a mound as is attested by the presence of Iron Age metalworking in the settling cone of the central pit. The importance of this site is that it demonstrates quite clearly that timber circles were in themselves monumental entities and that the circles alone would have been sufficient for the purposes of the celebrants: ceremonies could have been undertaken within the timber uprights irrespective of surrounding ditch or enclosure. While many form components of more complex monuments such as henges, the timber uprights were clearly capable of fulfilling ritual and religious requirements irrespective of their monumental peripheries. At Sarn-y-bryn-caled, the reason for the monument's simplicity must have been one of desire or

18   The timber circle at Sarn-y-bryn-caled during excavation (© CPAT).

intention since, in the ill-sorted gravels of the terraces of the River Severn, henge ditches could certainly have been constructed with comparative ease **(colour plate 4)**. Indeed, henge or henge-shaped monuments occur in close proximity to this timber circle at Coed-y-dinas, Dyffryn Lane and at the northern end of the Sarn-y-bryn-caled cursus, itself a monument which had already involved the excavation of over 1km of ditch, over 1000 tonnes of gravel and topsoil, and which thereby clearly demonstrates the technological capabilities of the local population.

Other freestanding circles occur at Ferrybridge where two circles, north and south, each with central postholes, occur within a ritual complex but without other monumental components in direct association **(fig 19)**. The double circles at Newgrange and Cocksbarrow also stood as distinct monuments and some other single and multiple pit circles have been recognised from aerial photographs. For example, a recent survey of aerial photographs in the Thames valley has identified freestanding pit circles at Radley and Eynsham **(fig 20)**. Both sites occur within areas of pits and ring-ditches and, while they cannot be proven to have held timber uprights (for only excavation can do this), nevertheless their morphology suggest that they may well have done. Aerial photographs of single pit circles are also known from Rearsby in Leicestershire and Withybushes in Pembrokeshire **(fig 21)**. These too are single entity sites without apparent monumental associations. Two multiple sites are well-known from Catholme, Barton-under-Needwood in Staffordshire **(fig 22)**. The northern of these monuments appears to be a complex site with perhaps four or five rings of pits radiating out from a central penannular ring-ditch which opens towards the east. The southern site appears to be a freestanding multiple site comprising five roughly concentric ovals around a large central space. There appears to be an entrance avenue marked by a splayed gap through the rings, once more

19 The Ferrybridge henge complex, Yorkshire (based on information supplied by J Hedges).

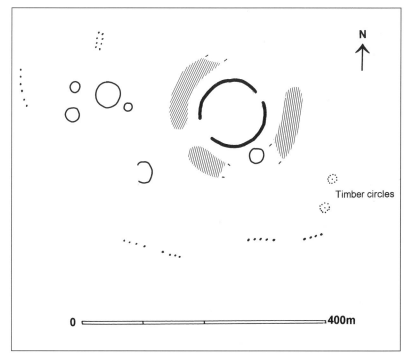

Timber circles

20   Pit circle in the Eynsham cemetery (RCHME, Crown copyright reserved).

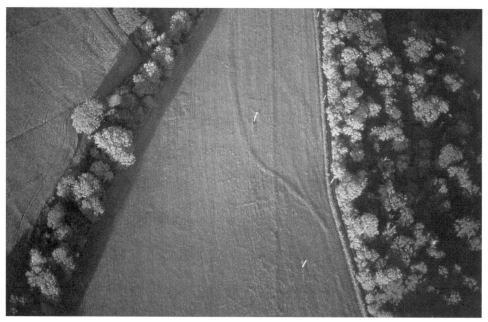

21   Withybush pit circle, Pembroke (photo Chris Musson, RCHAMW, Crown Copyright reserved).

22   Aerial photograph of the Catholme pit circles, Staffordshire. These sites are assumed to be multiple timber circles, but only excavation can prove this. (CUCAP aerial photograph No.BTL 095. By permission of CUCAP, copyright reserved.)

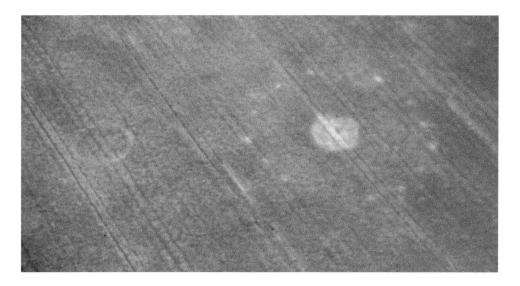

23   *Down Farm pit circle, Wiltshire. Despite the striking similarity of this site to the timber circle at Sarn-y-bryn-caled, excavation demonstrated that the pits of this circle never held posts (photo courtesy of Martin Green).*

to the east. Again it must be stressed that we cannot prove that these sites are timber circles, only excavation can conclusively demonstrate this, but the morphology of these cropmark sites with their obvious similarities to excavated examples, suggests that they are likely contenders. The large pit circle at Down Farm, Salisbury, however, serves as a cautionary note **(fig 23)**. This large single pit circle with central internal pit superficially resembled closely the cropmark photograph of Sarn-y-bryn-caled. Excavation has, however, demonstrated that the outer pits never held posts and that the inner pit contained a complex sequence of ritual activities including burial (inf. from Martin Green).

Timber circles may also be component sites to cursus monuments, henge monuments, stone circles, and barrows and, in these component sites, certain patterns can be recognised. For example, in cases where phasing can be determined, the timber circle seems to be primary and the orientation of the timber circle is usually different from that of the later monument. There are exceptions, however, and these may well be considered first.

Timber circles are found within cursus monuments at Dorchester-on-Thames and Springfield. At the latter site, the timber circle occupies the north-eastern end of the NE-SW orientated cursus **(fig 24)**. It lies close to the inside of the north-east terminal but only half of the monument was available for excavation since the south-west half was destroyed by a later drainage ditch. The circle is nevertheless centrally placed within the cursus and occupies virtually the whole of the monument's internal width. It appears to be part of the integral design of the cursus but it is difficult to determine whether the circle is primary or secondary within the construction sequence.

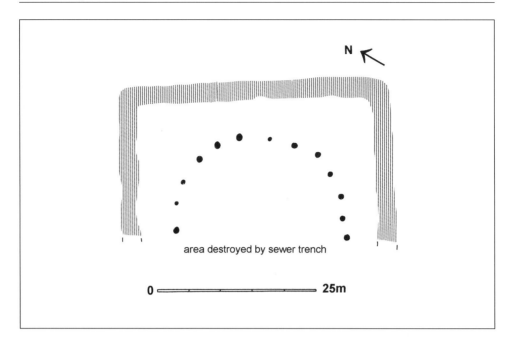

area destroyed by sewer trench

0 ———————————— 25m

24   *Plan of the Springfield timber circle set within the NE terminal of the cursus (after Hedges & Buckley).*

At Dorchester-on-Thames, the sequence of the cursus complex is better understood **(fig 25)**. The cursus itself appears to have been constructed in the quarter century prior to 3000BC. Two timber circles appear to have been constructed within the cursus possibly only slightly later. One, Site IV towards the north-west end of the monument, and the other, Site 3, towards the south-east end. Site IV is open to the east, aligned on the axis of the cursus while Site 3 has an egg-shaped plan with its longer axis similarly aligned. Interestingly, the penannular ring-ditches Sites V and VI which also date to this period and which may also have held posts in their initial phases, lie outside of the cursus and towards its north-west end. These sites also have their openings orientated on the axis of the monument, but point westwards rather than eastwards. Does this reflect a fundamental difference in the orientation of sites lying inside and outside the monument? Does this involve a difference in ritual between the sites which were included and those which were excluded? As mentioned above, we may here have sites which were used differently despite their morphological similarity.

The functions of cursus monuments are poorly understood. Their name, surviving in the archaeological record from their recognition in the eighteenth century when the antiquary, Stukeley, interpreted them as race tracks on the lines of Greek stadia, has served to embed in archaeological minds the notion that these sites were intended for procession and internal linear movement. They have fundamental differences from later avenues, however, and that is that unlike avenues, they are not open-ended. They are in effect enclosures, some remarkably long, with their ends closed by square or rounded terminal

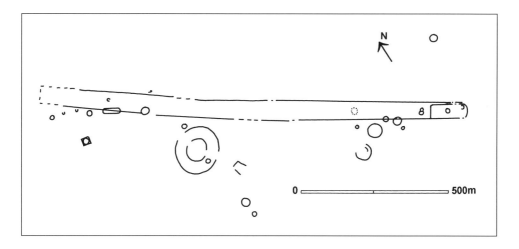

25   *Plan of the Dorchester-on-Thames cursus complex (after Bradley & Chambers).*

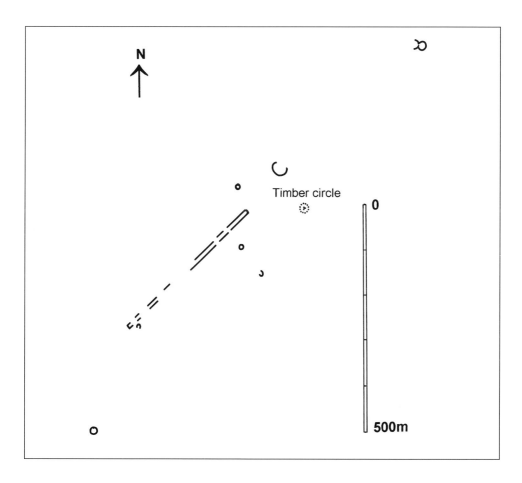

26   *Plan of the Sarn-y-bryn-caled cursus complex, Welshpool.*

ditches **(fig 26)**. People within the enclosure would indeed have had to move within its confines to visit sub-sites enclosed within its banks, but to suggest that these elongated enclosures were used for procession is to predate the Grand Old Duke of York by several millennia: once they had processed to one end, they would have to be marched down again. The causeways, often multiple, and frequently located in the lateral ditches, also preclude the notion of procession with no logical direction in which to turn first. It may be possible that the celebrants paraded around the enclosure, but almost certainly not through it. So, where timber circles within regular elongated enclosures can be dated, they appear to be secondary additions though not necessarily secondary by any great length of time and the data come only from a single cursus. What of their association with other enclosures?

The most notable are the large Wessex henges of Durrington Walls and Mount Pleasant where at neither site can a firm stratigraphical relationship between the circles and the enclosures be established, the circles being too distant from the earthworks, and the interiors being too eroded by natural and agricultural processes. At Durrington Walls, the excavations were undertaken at a time when C14 dating was relatively new and only three dates were obtained from the second phase of the southern circle, one from phase 1 of the southern circle and one from the northern circle as well as several from the enclosure ditch. With the exception of one date from the old ground surface beneath the bank, the dates obtained from the base of the enclosing ditch and from the timber circles are statistically identical centring on approximately 2500BC **(fig 27)**. But these dates suffer from large margins of error and on face value, phase 1 of the southern circle appears later than phase 2. This illustrates the danger of single radiocarbon dates. Could, for example, phase 1 of the southern circle actually pre-date the enclosure ditch? There are also two phases at the northern circle. Could phase 1 predate the henge here too? The orientations of the timber monuments do not really help. The screen and avenue associated with the northern circle are more or less due south from the circle and, if the avenue was extended, they would run well to the west of the southern enclosure entrance. The entrance of the southern circle does, however, open on to the main southern entrance of the henge **(fig 28)**. The northern circle is a simpler affair than the southern. Does this mean it is earlier? Or did it just serve a different purpose? Certainly Grooved Ware was recovered from the old ground surface below the bank of the main enclosure in the northern sector of Durrington Walls thus predating the henge's construction. It may well be therefore that there was a timber circle presence at Durrington walls before the main enclosure was constructed. Geophysical survey at Durrington Walls has also located curving anomalies which may well represent further circles in the interior. This leads to another unanswered question: is the enclosure at Durrington so large because it had a large number of earlier monuments to enclose? Without further excavation and a refined radiocarbon chronology, these questions must remain unanswered.

Similar questions may be asked at Mount Pleasant but once more answers do not readily present themselves. The contemporaneity of the timber circle with its surrounding enclosure has generally been accepted but once more although the radiocarbon dates suggest a broad contemporaneity they alone do not prove this given their margins of error. The northern entrance at the timber circle is in alignment with the northern entrance of

27 Radiocarbon dates for the timber circles at Durrington Walls.

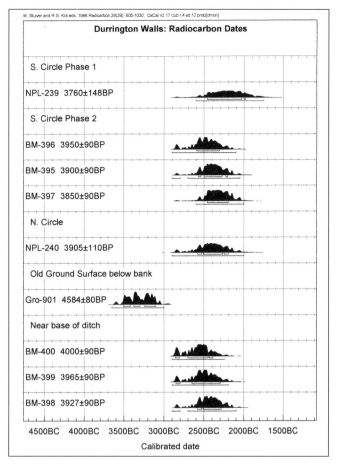

M. Stuiver and R.S. Kra eds. 1986 Radiocarbon 28(2B): 605-1030. OxCal v2.17 cub r:4 sd:12 prob[chron]

Durrington Walls: Radiocarbon Dates

S. Circle Phase 1

NPL-239 3760±148BP

S. Circle Phase 2

BM-396 3950±90BP

BM-395 3900±90BP

BM-397 3850±90BP

N. Circle

NPL-240 3905±110BP

Old Ground Surface below bank

Gro-901 4584±80BP

Near base of ditch

BM-400 4000±90BP

BM-399 3965±90BP

BM-398 3927±90BP

4500BC   4000BC   3500BC   3000BC   2500BC   2000BC   1500BC

Calibrated date

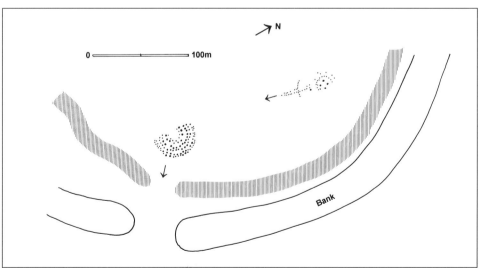

28   Plans of the northern and southern circles at Durrington Walls in relation to the nearest henge entrance (after Wainwright & Longworth).

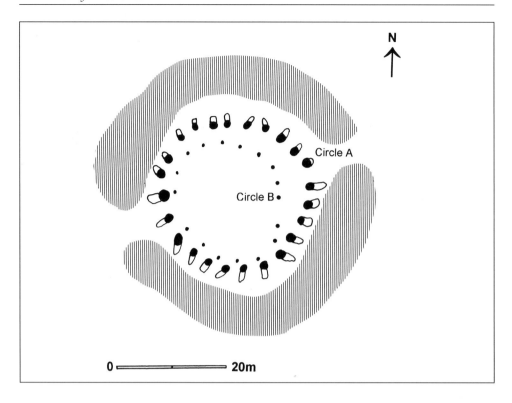

29   Plan of circles A and B at North Mains, Perthshire. Note the proximity of the post ramps of circle A to the henge ditch, itself truncated by agriculture (after Barclay).

the enclosure which may suggest that it is later than the main henge and aligned on it. The arguments are inconclusive.

The Wessex henges and the cursus monuments are large enclosures and rarely share recognisable stratigraphic relationships with the timber circles which they enclose. The smaller sites are more informative. Timber circles are often found within henges and the proximity of the henge ditch to the outermost uprights of the circles frequently preserves stratigraphic detail sufficient to reconstruct the site's constructional history. Where this is possible, the timber circle is usually the primary monument and indeed logic dictates this since it would be easier to manoeuvre these large timbers into place without the presence of a constraining earthwork.

This is certainly the case at Arminghall where the ramps dug to facilitate the setting of the posts face to the south and not towards the south-west-facing entrance. The radiocarbon dates and finds confirm this primacy and this is discussed in more detail below. At North Mains, the post ramps of the timber circle virtually encroach on the ditch and indeed, allowing for relatively recent erosion, the two features probably did coincide in places. This is certainly so in the eastern and western arcs **(fig 29)**. This means that the builders of the timber circle, had the henge already been in existence, would have had to stand in the ditch to erect the posts. Not only would this have been pretty undignified, but

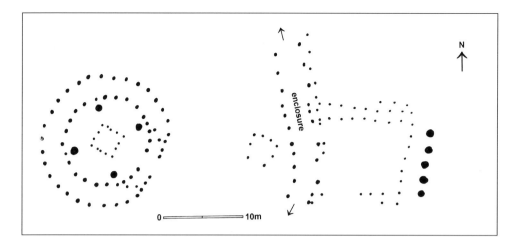

30   Ballynahatty, Co. Down. Plan of part of the enclosure and circle (after Hartwell).

it would also have presented a serious hindrance. The eccentric circle B at North Mains may be earlier still. This oval does not appear to relate to any of the henge's post-enclosure history and may therefore represent the earliest monumental phase, followed by circle A which may still have been extant when the henge ditch was constructed.

At Woodhenge, there is also evidence for the primacy of the wooden circle. The distribution of finds is discussed in chapter 5 below, but suffice it to say here that the pottery in particular was recovered from distinct deposits below the bank. Some of these ceramic concentrations also had cardinal locations in relation to the centre of the circles and it may therefore be logical to assume that the Grooved Ware is contemporary with the wooden rings and earlier than the henge. Once more, on a purely logical note, the henge ditch and bank could be seen as a distinct hindrance to the circle builders, restricting their movement and workspace. At Milfield North the timber circle unusually lies outside of the henge, unconstricted by the earthwork monument. However many of the postholes lie close to the outer edge of the ditch and, if the henge and circle coexisted, the posts would have to have protruded through the bank material. While not impossible, this theory appears to be unlikely as there is not the concentricity between the two monuments that one might expect had they coexisted. Again it would appear that the timber circle was the earlier component.

A type of monument that is receiving increasing attention in British Neolithic studies is the palisaded enclosure. These large sites are defined by perimeters of timber uprights and seem to appear in the archaeological record at about 3000 BC (Gibson 1998). They clearly involved substantial effort and human resources in their construction. The largest of these sites, at Hindwell in the Radnor Valley, mid-Wales, had a perimeter of over $1\frac{1}{2}$ miles (2.3km) and involved the setting of some 1400 oak posts each weighing about 4 tonnes. The other sites are more modest with areas averaging $7\frac{1}{2}$ acres (3ha) but would nevertheless have involved the felling, trimming, transportation and setting of substantial numbers of posts. Little work has been done on the interiors of these sites but there are tantalising traces of timber circles within many.

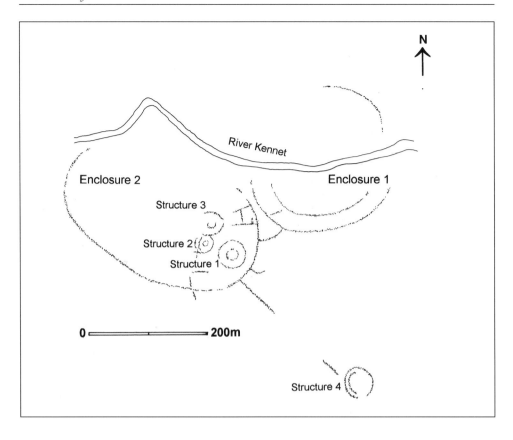

31   Plan of the West Kennet palisaded enclosure complex (after Whittle).

An enclosure defined by a double palisade is currently under excavation at Ballynahatty in the Lagan Valley, Co Down **(fig 30)**. This site lies within the Giant's Ring complex which is dominated by a large henge monument with internal passage grave, and the palisaded enclosure measures approx 100m long by 80m wide. At its eastern end lies a double timber circle 16m in diameter and surrounding a rectilinear setting of larger uprights. The circle has many features in common with that recently discovered at Knowth in Co. Meath and is interpreted by the excavator as a facaded timber enclosure surrounding a mortuary platform for the exposure and excarnation of the dead.

At Mount Pleasant, the multiple timber circle with cardinally orientated aisles lay within a palisade of close-set posts entered by access gaps flanked by truly monstrous oak posts some 2m in diameter and weighing an estimated 17 tonnes. The two entrances face north and east respectively and resemble the cardinal orientations of the aisles of the timber circle.

At West Kennet there are two juxtaposed palisaded sites **(fig 31)**. Like Mount Pleasant, they are composed of close-set contiguous timbers bedded within a palisade trench. The two enclosures are linked by strange connecting fencelines and the western of the two encloses multiple circular monuments including, in structure 2, a small inner circle of

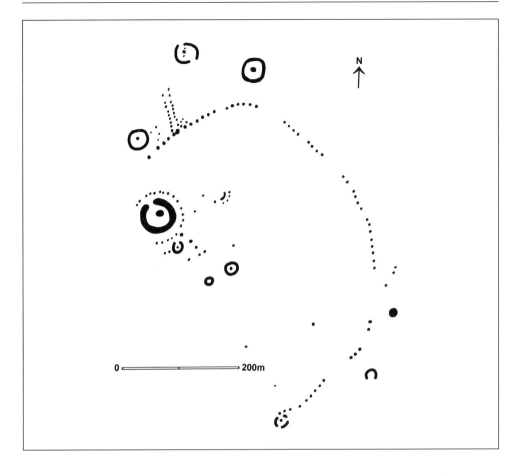

32   Plan of the Forteviot palisaded enclosure from aerial photographic transcriptions (after RCAHMS).

free-standing posts associated with Grooved Ware pottery **(colour plate 5).**

Certainly one and possibly two timber circles were located within the limited excavations at Meldon Bridge in Peeblesshire, a Neolithic promontory enclosure where a stout timber fence surrounded some 18 acres (8ha) in the angle between the Lyne Water and the Meldon Burn. Here feature K26 comprised a central pit containing the remains of a cremation and which was surrounded by a circle of small holes, possibly postholes. The other circle is more certain and comprised a circle of truncated postholes 9m in diameter set around a central post. Each posthole had contained a post of 15-20cm in diameter. Unfortunately neither setting was dated.

At other sites, air photographic evidence hints at the monuments inside. At Dunragit, Dumfries, a triple circuited palisaded enclosure appears to lie north-west of a large circle of pits, perhaps the remains of a timber circle. At Forteviot in Perthshire, a henge monument can be seen on aerial photographs to lie within an enclosure formed by individual post pits. Around this single-entranced Class I henge is a ring of dark spots

33   The timber circle and cairn at Oddendale, Cumbria, during excavation (courtesy of Percival Turnbull).

which may well represent the remains of a circle, which, like Milfield North, would be unusual in its situation outside of the henge **(fig 32)**. A large round barrow lying within the enclosure at Hindwell has yielded remarkable aerial photographs, indicating that it covers at least three concentric ring ditches and an innermost pit circle which it is tempting to consider as having originally held wooden uprights. Only excavation can prove the existence of timbers at these last three sites, but the evidence from the others, as well as from the perimeters themselves, clearly shows that Neolithic populations were exploiting their woodland resources to the full and were doubtless having a marked effect on their environments. It also provides testimony to the effectiveness of the stone axe.

Timber circles are also found in a variety of round barrow contexts. As with the henges, the timber circles tend to be primary though there are possible exceptions. At Oddendale, the double circle had ceased to be in use, the postholes had been sealed with stones amongst which were fragments of Beaker, and then a ring cairn had been constructed over the top **(fig 33)**. At Caebetin hill, the circle with its cardinal marker posts was covered by a substantial round barrow. A barrow also covered Whitton Hill and a ring cairn replaced Brenig 44, though the posts may have protruded through the bank. At Poole in Dorset **(fig 34)**, a small circle lay immediately within a penannular ring ditch. An avenue of posts ran through the causeway to the south-east and double posts were set in the north and south of the circle. The timber uprights were situated on the berm between the ditch and the barrow and as such this site and the protruding posts at Brenig 44 must have resembled the Dutch circle barrows quite closely.

At two other barrow sites, the timber circle lay outside of the ditch. Both these sites are late in the British sequence. Standlake 20 was regarded as Iron Age in date, though a re-

34   *Plan of the timber
      circle and barrow
      ditch at Poole, Dorset
      (after Case).*

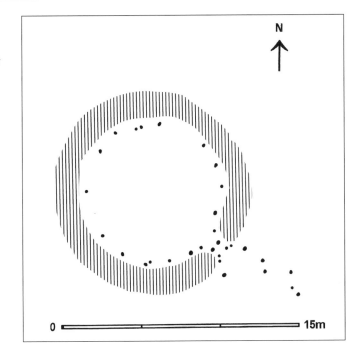

assessment of the pottery suggests middle Bronze Age, and the double circle at Ogden Down 3 with its avenue leading to the south was dated by radiocarbon to the later Bronze Age. It seems that at these last four sites at least, the timber circle was integral to the design of the cairn and at the last two it may even be a secondary element.

Perhaps the most enduring monumental transformation is where a timber circle is replaced in stone. In these cases, as might be expected, the timber circle is the primary monument and the stone circle later. This 'lithicisation' has taken place at a number of sites such as Balfarg, Croft Moraig, Machrie Moor XI, possibly Temple Wood, Stonehenge, the Sanctuary, Moncrieffe and possibly at Stanton Drew **(colour plate 6)**. At the Sanctuary the stones of the inner circle respect the postholes of ring C which has prompted some writers to suggest contemporaneity with the timber phase **(fig 35)**. If this is the case, then access to the inner rings would be denied for no gaps between the stones and the postholes appear to have been left and it seems more logical to assume that the monument was changed to a stone circle shortly after the timber monument fell into disuse, or was dismantled, but while the remains of the posts, perhaps their stumps or postholes, could still be seen. At Loch Roag, the early excavations depict an arc of charcoal-filled pits which it is tempting to think of as the remains of a timber circle, but the excavation report is lacking in precise detail **(fig 36)**.

At Stonehenge, a World Heritage site and arguably the most famous 'timber' circle of them all, there are internal timber settings as well as a possible circle represented by the Aubrey holes (named after the seventeenth-century antiquary John Aubrey). These latter features, which Atkinson regarded as ritual pits later reused as repositories for cremations, are now generally regarded to have originally held timber uprights which were removed prior to the insertion of the cremations (Cleal *et al.* 1995). The 56 Aubrey holes describe

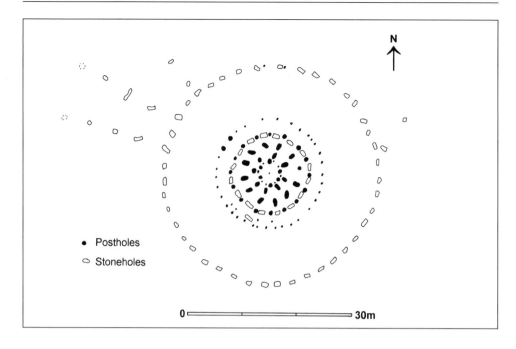

35   Plan of the Sanctuary, Wiltshire (after Cunnington).

a circle some 80m in diameter. The internal settings are more difficult to unravel and the ground-plan is not totally discernible due to later rebuilding and comparatively recent excavation. It appears, however, that the circle was a multiple one comprising at least six or seven rings of posts. The circles were approached by an avenue from the south which is cut by a screen. This posthole complex is clearly earlier than the sarsen and bluestone settings and dates to somewhere before 2600 BC **(fig 37)**. While the concentricity of the Aubrey holes and the internal circles with the main ditch and bank suggests that they are later or contemporary with the ditch, as does the orientation of the timber avenue with the southern entrance, unfortunately these timber phases cannot be dated. The one radiocarbon date from Aubrey hole 32 is from a cremation in the top of the fill, is therefore not primary, and, since the margin of error on this date is 275 years, the calibrated date range spans some two millennia.

   In all cases except Stonehenge, where the sarsens and bluestones are arranged as if in a timber setting, this replacement in stone must mark a fundamental change in the religious practices of the population. It is argued below that one of the functions of complex circle architecture is to exclude the uninitiated and maintain mysteries and secrets as the preserve of the few. Timber circles rarely afford views into their inner spaces. Stone circles, on the other hand, are open sites and while the standing stones may well have served as devices to define the inner space, they certainly did not deny visual access. Indeed the stones of some Welsh sites, for example, are so low as to be barely visible above the present-day peaty upland soils. Stone circles are not, therefore, as exclusive as timber ones and they serve to define space rather than enclose it.

36   *Stuart's 1876 engraving of the stone circle at Loch Roag. The possible earlier postholes are the dark patches marked 3-6 on the plan.*

Timber circles, then, are found in a variety of contexts within ritual landscapes and as components of more complex monument types. In the majority of cases they appear to be the primary component though there may have been a period of coexistence at some henge sites such as Balfarg and North Mains. Even at Woodhenge, sometimes regarded as a single-phase monument, there are good grounds for suggesting the primacy of the timber settings which may even have functioned in isolation for a considerable period, long enough for pottery deposits to be made, prior to the construction of the bank and ditch. These sequences point to a continuity of use of ritually or religiously significant places despite modifications to the architectural forms present and, doubtless, to the rituals practised.

37 Plan of the postholes (presumed phase 1) in the centre of Stonehenge and the avenue leading to the southern entrance. Compare this with the screen and avenue at the Northern Circle at Durrington Walls. The south-east arc suggests that up to 6 circles may have been present and that there may have been more than one phase (after Cleal et al).

3 The dating of timber circles

Timber circles are normally the plough-truncated remains of once splendid monuments. Rarely do they have any of their original contexts surviving; hardly at all are any old ground surfaces or contemporary environments preserved and what fragile remains might have existed have usually been removed by natural erosion and the effects of centuries of the scouring plough. So how do we know how old they are? Despite centuries of degradation there are often tell-tale traces, artefacts or contexts which might provide a clue as to the dates of these monuments. In the case of recently excavated examples, modern techniques such as radiocarbon measurement may be employed at sites where sufficient charcoal or associated organic remains survive, while at other sites associations may have either slipped into the postholes or have been placed in sealed environments. More rarely, on occasion, timber circles may be dated by stratigraphy in cases where the circle has more than one phase or is part of a more complex site history. Some examples of this have already been mentioned in the previous chapter. Rarely are all three techniques available at any particular site and each dating technique is itself fraught with difficulties.

Absolute dating techniques, and in particular radiocarbon dating, which provide calendar date ranges for these sites should in theory be the most accurate method of determining the age of a timber circle but, for dates to be reliable, great care needs to be taken with regard to the derivation of the sample and its relationship to the erection of the monument. For example, charcoal dates the death of the wood from which it is derived and not necessarily the erection of the monument. In some cases where the wood is oak, the sample may come from the heartwood of the tree which may already have been as much as 500 years old or even older when the tree was felled. As a result, the date obtained from this sample would be 500 years older than the date for the building of the circle. Similarly, charcoal from the filling of the posthole, despite its context, may not be contemporary with the construction phase of the monument. The digging of the postholes in, for example, the late Neolithic may have chopped through an early Neolithic hearth and this older material may have become incorporated into the post packing. Using this sample, the timber circle may well appear to have an early Neolithic date. This example is extreme, but places of ritual attention frequently enjoy considerable longevity and other ritual fires may well have existed on site prior to the monumentalisation of the sacred place. This residual charcoal, therefore, can at best only provide a *terminus post quem*, or date after which the site was built. This *terminus post quem* may be hours or years or decades or even centuries earlier than the actual building of the circle.

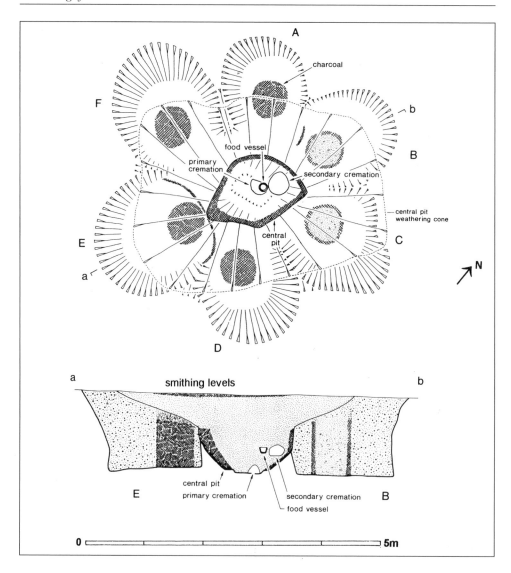

38   Plan and section of the inner circle at Sarn-y-bryn-caled, Powys. Note the Iron Age smithing levels in the top of the central pit (drawing by Brian Williams, © CPAT).

Another problem potentially exists. That is, where a circle has at its centre or within its interior a feature such as a hearth, it cannot always be proven beyond inference or reasonable doubt that the two features are contemporary. Logic might dictate that they are, but equally the coincidence may be fortuitous or a result of the longevity of ritual sites mentioned above. A case in point is the Iron Age bronze smithing within the central pit of the Sarn-y-bryn-caled circle **(fig 38).** It was fortunate in this case that resources were available in the post-excavation phase to test the burnt clay for metallurgical residues, to date the clay by thermoluminescence, to radiocarbon date the associated charcoal and to have the bronze casting waste analysed for chemical content. Together these techniques unravelled the questions of chronology: the fired clay contained no metallurgical residues and resulted from the burning down of the circle since it produced a Bronze Age thermoluminescent date, but the chemical composition of the bronze and the radiocarbon date from the charcoal attested Iron Age bronze smithing which had clearly been undertaken in the weathering cone of the central pit of an early Bronze Age ritual monument.

Sufficient attention has not always been paid to these details or pitfalls of chronology and consequently the radiocarbon dates obtained for timber circles (or indeed any archaeological monument type) need to be arranged into three main categories; direct association, indirect association and *terminus ante/post quem* (the date before or after which the main features must have been deposited). In addition there are problem dates which appear not to fit the other archaeological data and still other dates which may be rejected as chronologically meaningless. In what follows, all radiocarbon dates are expressed in calibrated form (that is in calibrated calendar years BC as opposed to radiocarbon years) unless otherwise specified.

The first category of dates, those directly associated with the circles, are clearly the most accurate and informative **(fig 39)**. They reliably indicate the currency of timber circles from c.2800-1000 BC. This date range is confirmed by the less reliable indirectly associated dates which actually extend the date-bracket somewhat to 3000-900 BC though this may be a result of the diminishing reliability of the samples **(fig 40)**. For example, the early dates come from Balfarg where the charcoal was derived from the backfilled packing material in the post-holes and therefore possibly pre-dates the construction of the timber monument by an unknown amount of time. The *termini ante quos* dates again fall within the brackets already established.

Examples of problem dates come from two early excavations at Arminghall and Bleasdale. At the latter site, waterlogged wood was dated in 1964, some 30 years after the excavation, but the provenance of the wood is in doubt; did it come from the outer palisade, from the inner timber circle or from the base of the penannular ditch ? We are unlikely to find out and therefore the date is useless. With regards to Arminghall, the date of c.3500-2700 BC is considerably earlier than the primary rusticated Beaker associations from the ditch even allowing for the effect of old wood from the oak posts. However, it is likely that the timber horseshoe here predates the henge monument (see below) and therefore the date may be accepted and, if so, confirms that the timber circle predates the henge monument, perhaps by a considerable degree.

The combined radiocarbon evidence, despite its pitfalls and limitations, does however provide a chronological bracket into which to fit timber circles. It suggests that the monument type had a currency of over 2000 years spanning the later Neolithic and earlier Bronze Age with a 'tailing off' into the later Bronze Age.

With regard to associated artefacts, secure associations with timber circles are few. Once more particular attention has to be paid to the context of the finds and their true relationship with the circle. For example, the western Neolithic sherds from Croft Moraig **(fig 41)** were originally considered by the excavators to have been residual at this complex site and were regarded as providing only a *terminus post quem* for the timber circle.

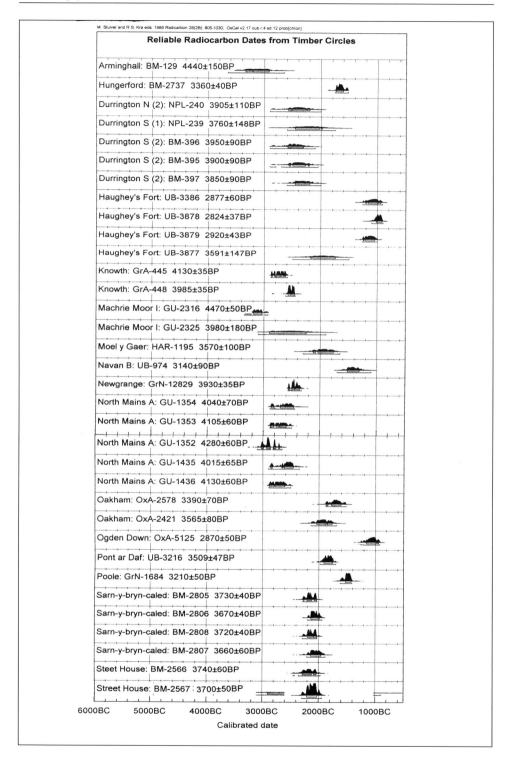

M. Stuiver and R.S. Kra eds. 1986 Radiocarbon 28(2B): 805-1030; OxCal v2.17 cub r 4 sd:12 prob[chron]

Reliable Radiocarbon Dates from Timber Circles

Arminghall: BM-129 4440±150BP

Hungerford: BM-2737 3360±40BP

Durrington N (2): NPL-240 3905±110BP

Durrington S (1): NPL-239 3760±148BP

Durrington S (2): BM-396 3950±90BP

Durrington S (2): BM-395 3900±90BP

Durrington S (2): BM-397 3850±90BP

Haughey's Fort: UB-3386 2877±60BP

Haughey's Fort: UB-3878 2824±37BP

Haughey's Fort: UB-3879 2920±43BP

Haughey's Fort: UB-3877 3591±147BP

Knowth: GrA-445 4130±35BP

Knowth: GrA-448 3985±35BP

Machrie Moor I: GU-2316 4470±50BP

Machrie Moor I: GU-2325 3980±180BP

Moel y Gaer: HAR-1195 3570±100BP

Navan B: UB-974 3140±90BP

Newgrange: GrN-12829 3930±35BP

North Mains A: GU-1354 4040±70BP

North Mains A: GU-1353 4105±60BP

North Mains A: GU-1352 4280±60BP

North Mains A: GU-1435 4015±65BP

North Mains A: GU-1436 4130±60BP

Oakham: OxA-2578 3390±70BP

Oakham: OxA-2421 3565±80BP

Ogden Down: OxA-5125 2870±50BP

Pont ar Daf: UB-3216 3509±47BP

Poole: GrN-1684 3210±50BP

Sarn-y-bryn-caled: BM-2805 3730±40BP

Sarn-y-bryn-caled: BM-2806 3670±40BP

Sarn-y-bryn-caled: BM-2808 3720±40BP

Sarn-y-bryn-caled: BM-2807 3660±60BP

Steet House: BM-2566 3740±60BP

Street House: BM-2567 3700±50BP

6000BC   5000BC   4000BC   3000BC   2000BC   1000BC

Calibrated date

39   Reliable radiocarbon dates from timber circles.

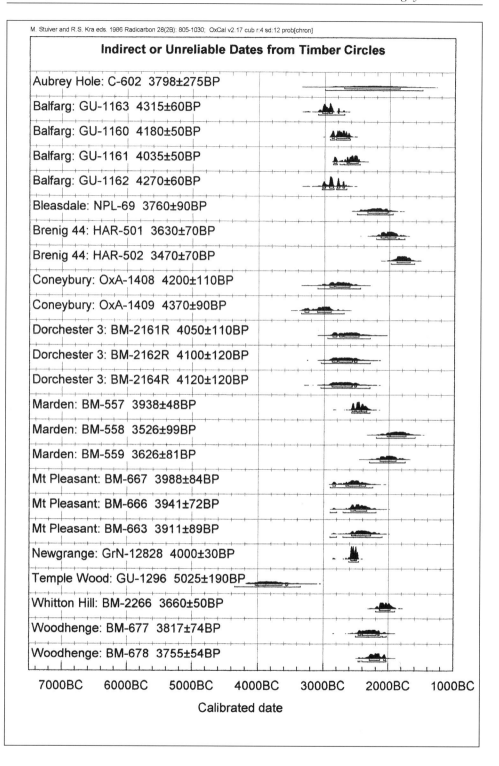

M. Stuiver and R.S. Kra eds. 1986 Radicarbon 28(2B): 805-1030; OxCal v2.17 cub r:4 sd:12 prob[chron]

Indirect or Unreliable Dates from Timber Circles

Aubrey Hole: C-602 3798±275BP

Balfarg: GU-1163 4315±60BP

Balfarg: GU-1160 4180±50BP

Balfarg: GU-1161 4035±50BP

Balfarg: GU-1162 4270±60BP

Bleasdale: NPL-69 3760±90BP

Brenig 44: HAR-501 3630±70BP

Brenig 44: HAR-502 3470±70BP

Coneybury: OxA-1408 4200±110BP

Coneybury: OxA-1409 4370±90BP

Dorchester 3: BM-2161R 4050±110BP

Dorchester 3: BM-2162R 4100±120BP

Dorchester 3: BM-2164R 4120±120BP

Marden: BM-557 3938±48BP

Marden: BM-558 3526±99BP

Marden: BM-559 3626±81BP

Mt Pleasant: BM-667 3988±84BP

Mt Pleasant: BM-666 3941±72BP

Mt Pleasant: BM-663 3911±89BP

Newgrange: GrN-12828 4000±30BP

Temple Wood: GU-1296 5025±190BP

Whitton Hill: BM-2266 3660±50BP

Woodhenge: BM-677 3817±74BP

Woodhenge: BM-678 3755±54BP

7000BC   6000BC   5000BC   4000BC   3000BC   2000BC   1000BC

Calibrated date

40   *Less reliable dates from timber circles.*

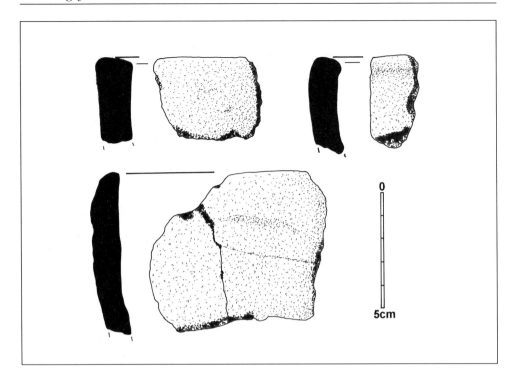

41   Earlier Neolithic pottery from Croft Moraig, Perthshire (after Piggot & Simpson).

Nevertheless, it is also possible that the intricate and long-lived site history may in fact suggest that the sherds are indeed associated with the first phase of the site and therefore date the timber circle to sometime before 3000 BC. Plain bowl pottery, including one lugged sherd, was also residual at Cairnpapple Hill though fragments of bone pins, regarded as the remains of stylistically later Neolithic skewer pins, but on flimsy evidence, were more securely associated. Grimston Ware also came from the possible timber circle at Oakham and early-middle Neolithic Mildenhall style pottery was recovered from the pit circles at Maxey. These early associations may suggest that the genesis of circle building, timber as well as stone, evolved in the latter part of the fourth millennium BC.

Whilst these early associations are both tentative and rare, middle and later Neolithic artefacts are more common. Middle Neolithic Peterborough Ware sherds, from highly decorated thick-walled, heavy-rimmed, round-based bowls, were found at Conygar Hill but this is as yet unpublished in detail. Peterborough sherds from elaborate Mortlake style vessels were found at Dorchester V and VI but from secondary contexts in the pit fills providing *termini ante quos* dates for the monuments. Peterborough Ware (Mortlake and Fengate styles) and some Beaker sherds were recovered from the excavations at Springfield from near-primary contexts (inf. J. Hedges) and both Peterborough and Grooved Ware were both recovered from Whitton Hill though in view of recent radiocarbon trends for these ceramic types, they are unlikely to be exactly contemporary. Grooved Ware came from the ring-ditch and the subsoil while the Peterborough was

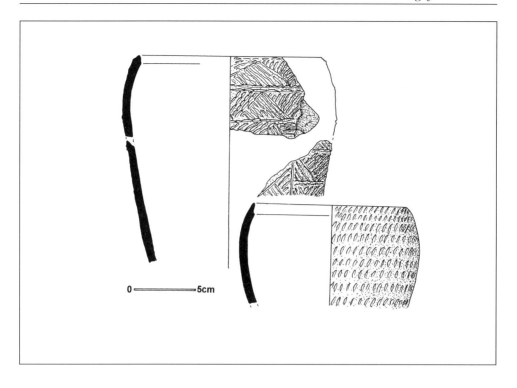

42   Grooved Ware from the timber circles at Durrington Walls South (upper) and Lawford (after Wainwright & Longworth and Lawson et al.).

associated with the central cremation. This important and rare find of Peterborough Ware in a sepulchral context cannot be directly associated with either the timber circle or the ring-ditch but in the absence of earlier or later finds from the site, its association with pre-ring-ditch features may possibly be assumed. The associated radiocarbon date of c.2000-1400 BC is however too old for the general range of Peterborough dates and may raise the question of ceramic identification.

A more common ceramic association with timber circles is Grooved Ware (**fig 42**). This sometimes plain but often highly decorated flat-based ceramic occurs at 16 sites and most notably at the large, elaborate, complex circles. These are the large Wessex sites of Durrington Walls, Mount Pleasant and Marden as well as the Sanctuary, Woodhenge, and multi-ringed complexes further afield such as Balfarg. At Woodhenge, the Grooved Ware comes from the henge ditch, particularly the eastern terminal, and was stratigraphically below Beaker sherds. Much pottery also came from the old ground surface below the bank, particularly in the southern sector (**fig 43**). Few pieces of ceramic came from the post-holes. At this site at least the Grooved Ware appears to be contemporary with the construction of the circles and earlier than the henge though doubtless it was also contemporary with the use of the total monument. Other Grooved Ware associated sites are Balfarg, Dorchester 3, Machrie Moor I, West Kennet, Ballynahatty and Knowth at which sites the pottery came from the post-holes and often in considerable quantities. At

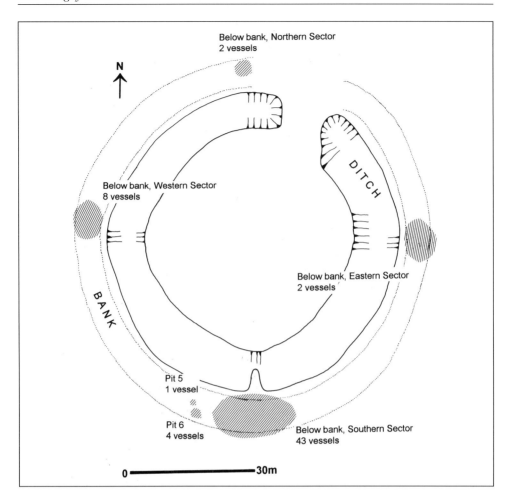

Below bank, Northern Sector
2 vessels

N

DITCH

Below bank, Western Sector
8 vessels

BANK

Below bank, Eastern Sector
2 vessels

Pit 5
1 vessel

Pit 6
4 vessels

Below bank, Southern Sector
43 vessels

0 ══════════════ 30m

43   *The distribution of the pottery from pre-henge contexts around Woodhenge. The broad cardinal locations, mirrored in the timber circles, suggest that the timber circles may pre-date the henge.*

Ballynahatty and Knowth in particular, a distinctive insular style of Grooved Ware, almost totally restricted to Ireland, seems to have been deliberately tipped into the post packing and must doubtlessly be regarded as 'ritually charged'. Grooved Ware was recovered from the ditch and the interior of the site at Lawford, from the ditches at Coneybury, Moncreiffe and Whitton Hill. Grooved Ware was recovered from the palisaded circle at Street House, a peculiar site which cannot really be paralleled anywhere in Britain and whose incorporation in a corpus of timber circles is only because it does not readily fall into any other monument category.

Beaker pottery has been recovered from 15 timber circles including Newgrange and Arminghall where rusticated Beaker was recovered from the ditch and which provides a *terminus ante quem* for the timber circle. This is also the case for the handled Beaker from the central grave at Balfarg which post-dates the construction of the circle. The funerary

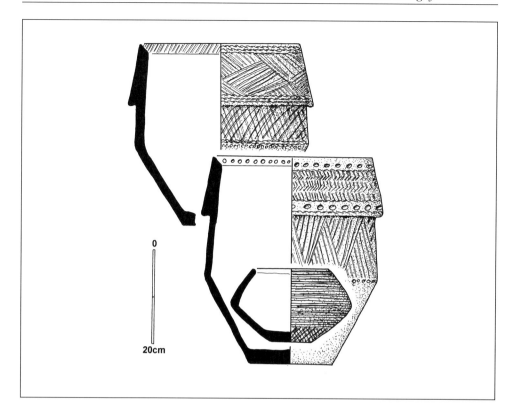

44   The collared urns and miniature vessel from Bleasdale (after Varley).

Beaker from North Mains, the corded Beaker from the cairn at Oddendale, and the Beaker from secondary contexts at Coneybury also provide little more than *termini ante quos* for these sites. Beaker was unusually found at Durrington Walls North Circle (II) and South Circle (II) and at the Sanctuary (though largely from the later stone-holes) in contexts which suggested contemporaneity with at least part of the use of the circles and in otherwise overwhelmingly Grooved Ware assemblages. At Mount Pleasant and Marden the Beaker sherds were not in primary contexts. Beaker sherds were found in the upper (and therefore secondary) levels of the postholes B6, C5 and C9 at Woodhenge, associated with Grooved Ware at Moncrieffe, came from Pit C at Milfield North, Northumberland and from the old ground surface below the ring cairn at Oddendale. It was also found in the stones sealing the disused post-pits at this site and once more provides little more than a *terminus ante quem* for the timber circle.

Twelve timber circles may be dated by early Bronze Age associations. A multiple Collared Urn deposit accompanied by a small accessory vessel or 'pigmy cup' were in the central grave at Bleasdale (**fig 44**) though there is no stratigraphy to relate this burial phase to the construction of the monument. Collared Urns also provide *termini ante quos* for Brenig 44, Goldington and Litton Cheney. Food Vessel associations are also rare but once more provide *termini ante quos* in the form of a Food Vessel Urn in the barrow covering the

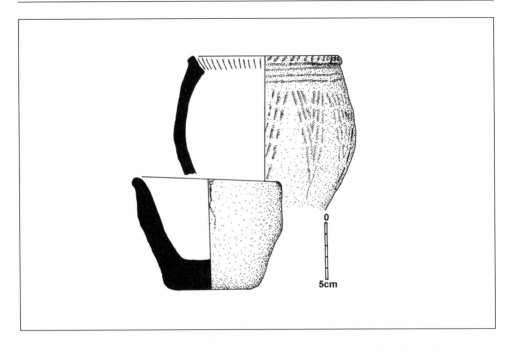

45   *The Food Vessels from Milfield North (upper) and Sarn-y-bryn-caled. Both vessels are secondary to the timber circles (Milfield after Harding).*

timber circle at Caebetin Hill and Food Vessel burials from Milfield North and Sarn-y-bryn-caled where, despite their central positions, neither can be related to the construction phases of the circles (**fig 45**). Elaborately decorated pigmy cups were, however, found in a primary position at Hungerford and in secondary positions at Oddendale and Bleasdale as mentioned above. A Camerton-Snowshill dagger provides a *terminus ante quem* date for Caerloggas I and barbed and tanged arrowheads provide similar dating at Milfield North and Sarn-y-bryn-caled (**colour plate 14**).

With regard to individual site stratigraphy, timber circles are difficult to date, but occasionally this is possible on sites where building sequences can be identified, for example where later postholes cut earlier ones, or where the circles form components or precursors of other monuments, for example components of henges or pre-barrow structures. Building sequences are difficult to identify in concentric sites but nevertheless clear phases have been identified at Durrington Walls North and South (**fig 46**). In the case of component monuments, it is often difficult to determine where the timber circle should fit within the site's history. At Milfield North the timber circle lies outside the henge and clearly predates the class II monument since some of the postholes underlie the presumed line of the external bank (**fig 47**). At Arminghall the radiocarbon dates from the timber uprights predate by a considerable period the primary associations in the henge ditch. However the primacy of the timber setting can be demonstrated in other ways. The substantial post ramps used for sliding the massive oak posts into their sockets, all face south yet the entrance to the monument is to the south-west. These south-pointing ramps

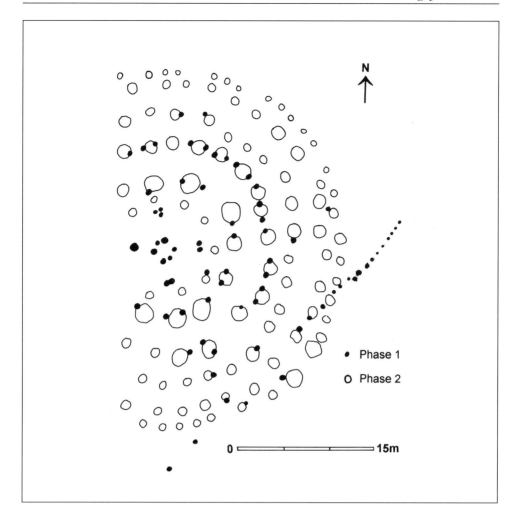

N

• Phase 1

O Phase 2

0 ⊏━━━━━━━━━━━⊐ 15m

46   *Phases 1 and 2 of the Durrington Walls Southern Circle (after Wainwright & Longworth).*

suggest that the trees were brought from this direction and thus would have had to cross the line of the ditches and bank, were they already in existence. Furthermore, in the southern arc, the edges of the post ramps are so close to the inside edge of the ditch that, had the ditch existed at the time when the uprights were erected, problems would surely have been caused during the setting of the posts with the circle builders having to stand in or over the wide inner ditch (**fig 48**). In this case at least the timber monument must have been earlier and the henge the secondary monument. A similar case was used to argue the primacy of timber circle A at North Mains where, like Arminghall, the edges of the post ramps are so close to the inner edge of the ditch that co-existence cannot realistically be considered (**fig 49**).

In these three sites at least, the timber circles pre-dated henges though there may have been an element of co-existence at Arminghall, and there was certainly such at North

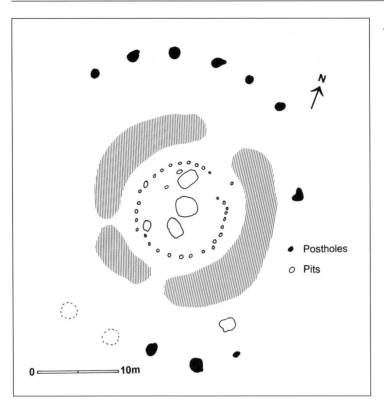

47 *Milfield North, Northumberland. The postholes on the east side in particular would have lain under the henge bank (after Harding).*

● Postholes

○ Pits

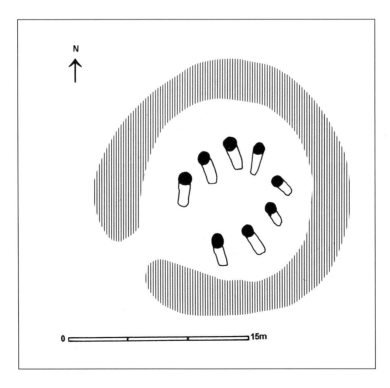

48 *Arminghall, Norfolk. The directions of the postramps indicate that the entrance to the henge was unlikely to have been utilised during the erection of the timber uprights. The posts all appear to have been brought from the south-east (after Clark).*

49   Aerial photograph of North Mains during excavation (courtesy of Gordon Barclay; Crown Copyright: Historic Scotland).

Mains. There appears to have been no such co-existence at Milfield North, however, where the henge seems to have replaced the circle which partially underlay the presumed line of the bank, though admittedly the evidence is very scant.

At other sites, the primary timber circles may be replaced in stone again adding a stratigraphic dimension to the sites' histories. Sites which demonstrate this 'lithicisation' are Croft Moraig, Moncreiffe, Balfarg, Temple Wood, Machrie Moor, Cairnpapple, the Sanctuary, possibly at Loch Roag, and, most famous and dramatic of all, Stonehenge.

The writer knows of no instances of the reverse sequence, from stone to timber, though this is hardly to be expected and is doubtlessly a direct result of the durability of stone. This does not mean, however, that we must regard timber circles as the precursors of stone circles in any but the most general of terms since both monument types can be demonstrated to have the same period of currency. Indeed, when discussing the link between stone circles and those of wood, Mercer has suggested that ring A at Balfarg might have been related to the recumbent stone circles of Aberdeenshire some 45 miles (70km) to the north (**colour plate 7**). This was deduced from the estimated heights of the timbers, as calculated from the depths of the postholes, which indicated that the timbers appeared to be graduated in length (and thus also in height) so that the lowest posts were opposite the highest in the circle. In this way too are the stones of recumbent stone circles downwardly graded in height away from the recumbent stone. Attractive though this idea is, it must remain only a possibility: the postholes at Balfarg were extremely eroded and thus the heights of the posts were difficult to estimate, there are no other similar parallels, even in Aberdeenshire the main centre for recumbent stone circles, and stone circles generally do not mimic their timber counterparts in terms of layout or spacing.

Common to many timber circles is their use for burial and/or their replacement by barrows and cairns but rarely can this sepulchro-ritual activity be shown to be contemporary with the construction of the monument. At Balfarg and North Mains, for example, both sites received Beaker and Food Vessel burials in their later phases. At Goldington and Litton Cheney burials associated with Collared Urns were secondary to the timber circles. Cremation burials were also placed in the redundant post-pits at Dorchester 3 after the posts had been removed and this may also have been the case at Dorchester IV-VI where posts appear to have been dug out. By extension of the hypothesis, a similar explanation might be suggested for the Aubrey holes of Stonehenge and thus explain the cremations centrally placed in the upper fills of these much discussed but poorly understood pits. These cremations, however, appear to be later Neolithic rather than Bronze Age and are associated with bone pins and artefacts generally associated with Grooved Ware.

Brenig 44, Oddendale and Cocksbarrow were all replaced by Bronze Age ring cairns, with burials still later at Brenig. Poole, Caebetin, possibly Ogden Down 3, Standlake, and Lawford were all covered by round barrows and with Bronze Age burials at all but Standlake. Cairnpapple, Moncreiffe and Croft Moraig were similarly covered by later round cairns. The sealing of a now redundant monument in this way and its change of use towards a sepulchral function once more reflects a pattern seen at stone circles where burials appear to be later and which are often incorporated in or are covered by mounds. This further strengthens the links between the two classes of monument.

When the size and complexity of timber circles is viewed against date, a pattern emerges (**fig 50**). Sometime just before 3000BC small-diameter, unelaborate timber circles like Croft Moraig, Whitton Hill and the massive-posted but modest-diametered Arminghall enter the archaeological record. Their origins are obscure and their antecedents difficult to trace but they reflect a general change to regular circularity in the ritual monuments around this time. In the centuries either side of 2500 BC, there develop the large complex timber circles like Durrington Walls, Balfarg, Woodhenge and the Sanctuary, representing the climax of timber circle architecture and supremely represented by the sarsen circle and horseshoe at Stonehenge where contemporary timber circle design became fossilised in stone. After 2000 BC, timber circles decline in both complexity and diameter mirroring the pattern for their lithic counterparts. They become increasingly focused on burials and become integral to or replaced by funerary monuments in much the same way as later stone circles. Hungerford and, later still, Ogden Down at the end of the range of both time and scale resemble in their modesty Whitton Hill and Croft Moraig almost two millennia earlier. Timber circles take more or less a complete millennium to fade from the archaeological record in Britain though their legacy might well live on elsewhere.

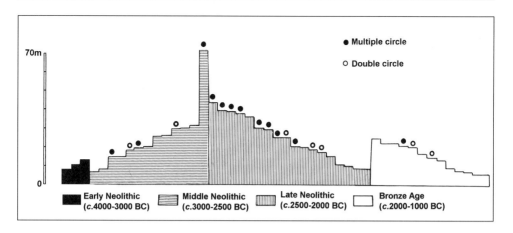

50   Diagrammatic summary of the chronology of British timber circles set against diameter and complexity. The later Neolithic certainly appears to see the climax of the timber circle tradition.

Some Irish sites warrant special mention at this point and in particular Navan, Knockaulin, Raffin, Lugg and Haughey's Fort. At first glance, these sites do not seem to fit the proposed chronological scheme suggested above yet the five concentric circles of the multiple circular site at Navan (**fig 51**) bear close comparison with the complex Grooved Ware associated sites of the British sequence and were, like many British sites, sealed by a large cairn. The Navan monument had an entrance aisle opening to the west along which a large central post was back-breakingly dragged and heaved upright into a deep pit by means of a ramp 6m long. From the depth of the pit, this post could have stood up to 13m high. The uprights of the main wall were linked by horizontal split timbers thus obscuring the interior as has been suggested above for some British sites. Navan, however, is about two millennia later than the comparable British sites, with a dendrochronological date of *c.*100 BC from the central post. The second site, Knockaulin, is more complex than Navan in terms of its phasing and structural elements but is also Iron Age in date (**fig 52**). In its second phase, broadly contemporary with Navan, it appeared as an outer palisaded ringwork around a central tower. Freestanding posts encircled this tower and are interpreted as having been joined by lintels. At Raffin, a multiple timber circle was overlain by a later Bronze Age house which acts as a *terminus ante quem* and at Lugg, the once more multiple circle complete with avenue to the north, henge-like ditch and posthole pairs interpreted as lintel-bearing trilithon-like arrangements (trixylons?) produced later Bronze Age pottery from posthole 17 but is otherwise undated. At Haughey's Fort, a large double circle with an outer diameter of 25m has been radiocarbon dated to 1260-950 BC while in Britain the double circle of Ogden Down is broadly contemporary. Standlake 20 in Oxfordshire (**fig 53**) lies outside but concentric with a ring ditch which was dated by analogy to the earlier Bronze Age despite the presence of reported Iron Age pottery from low in the ditch silts. However, recent analysis of the pottery has identified it as middle Bronze Age rather than Iron Age and thus is must be broadly contemporary with Ogden Down. These sites on the British side of the

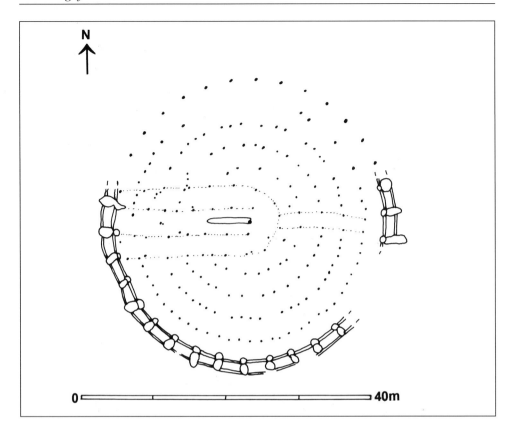

51   Plan of the Iron Age multiple timber circle at Navan, Co Armagh (after Lynn).

Irish Sea combined with Haughey's Fort and Raffin serve to extend rather than radically alter the chronological scheme. These circles, despite their superficial resemblance to the British sites warn against over-reliance on typological similarity.

The later Irish material does pose an obvious question. To what extent are the timber circles of the British and Irish sequences related given their chronological disparity? Their groundplans are so similar that it is difficult to deny a relationship, even a common ancestry. In Britain there are Neolithic and Bronze Age examples but as yet none can be assigned to the Iron Age. In Ireland, examples are present from all three periods. Did the tradition continue in Ireland? Was there an attempt to revive the tradition in the final centuries BC? Or did some other stimulus prompt a powerful priesthood to resurrect some earlier practices, knowledge of which survived in folk tradition and oral histories?

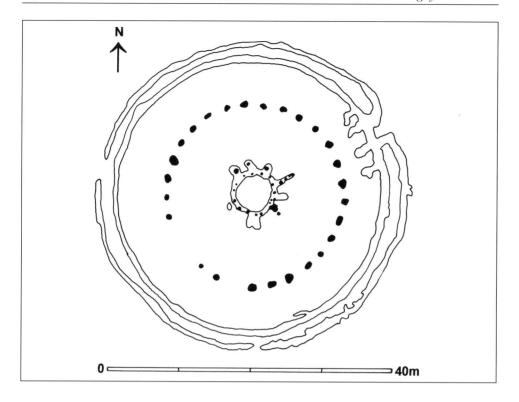

52   *Plan of the complex timber setting at Knockaulin, Co. Kildare (after Lynn).*

53 *Plan of Standlake 20.*
A re-examination of
the pottery suggests that
this site may be earlier
than previously thought
and it therefore is
closely comparable with
Ogden Down (after
Catling).

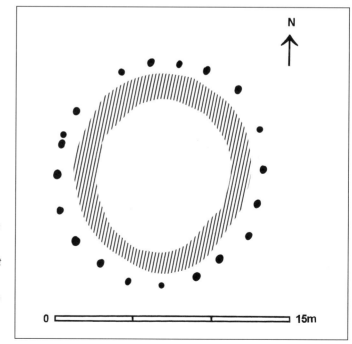

4 Timber circles in Europe

Elsewhere on the European landmass, timber circles are somewhat different to their British counterparts in both arrangement and date. With some notable exceptions, they tend to comprise solid palisades rather than spaced postholes but both single and multiple variants are encountered and they also span the Neolithic and Bronze Age. It is in the Netherlands that the closest parallels for the British material can be found in terms of both appearance and date.

Behrens (1981) published 'the first Woodhenge' in central Europe in *Antiquity*. The similarity with Woodhenge was a distant one save that the site in question at Quenstedt, near Halle, was a multiple timber enclosure. It lay on a south-west-pointing spur and comprised five broadly concentric and roughly oval palisades **(fig 54)**. The overall maximum diameter of the site was in the region of 80m and the area enclosed by the innermost palisade was approximately 45m by 35m. There are three coinciding entrances through all the palisades, one to the north-west, one to the south-south-east and the third just north of east. At these entrances, the palisades are inturned in many cases though the third entrance in the south-south-east is marked by two postholes which doubtless formed some sort of gated structure. It was suggested at the time, though not convincingly, that the north-west and east-north-east entrances were orientated on the summer solstice sunsets and sunrises respectively though no such orientation could be assigned the south-eastern causeway. Recent radiocarbon dates from this site suggest a date of 4500 BC.

In the description of Quenstedt, analogy was drawn with another palisade circle at Tesetice Kyjovice in Moravia **(fig 55)**. This oval site was surrounded by a wide ditch with cardinally orientated entrances. The ditch enclosed an area approximately 55m east-west by 45m north-south. Within this enclosure was a double palisade, the two elements separated by some 5m. The entrances through the palisades coincided with those of the ditch and the cardinal orientations of these were doubtless intentional.

Other ceremonial circles have been found at a number of sites. In Bavaria, the staff of the Bayerisches Landesamt für Denkmalpflege have been investigating several such sites including a double ditched enclosure at Viecht-Eching (Becker 1996). With a diameter of almost 70m. The Viecht-Eching site has a double-ditched perimeter 10m apart. There are also traces on the geophysical survey of subsidiary internal circles showing as weaker anomalies than the main perimeters **(fig 56)**. These are doubtless to be interpreted as the traces of a double internal palisade truncated by erosion resulting from its hilltop position. There are coinciding entrances through the ditches to the south-south-east and traces of

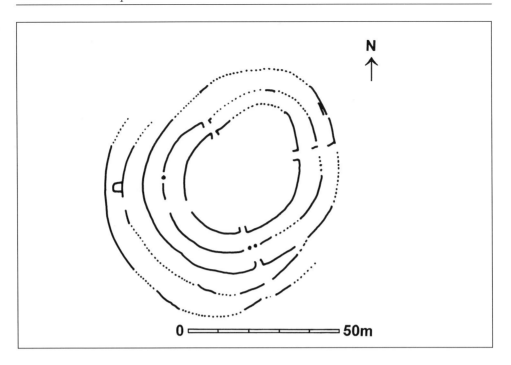

54   Quenstedt (after Petrasch).

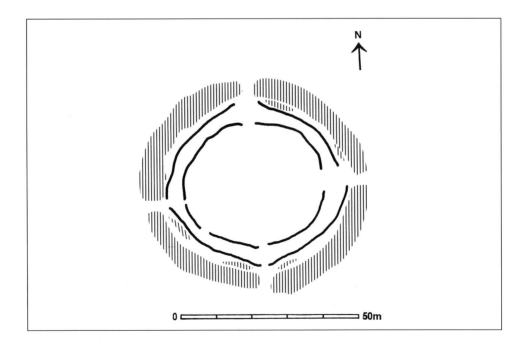

55   Plan of Tesetice (after Petrasch).

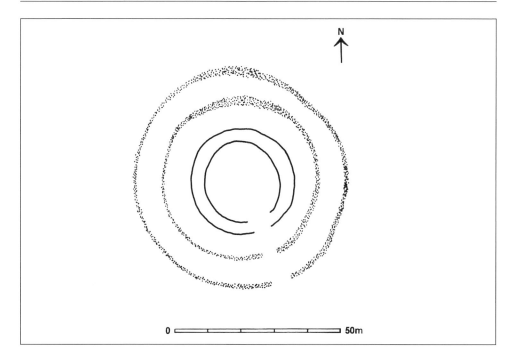

56   *Plan of Viecht Eching (after Petrasch).*

a possible north-north-west gap in the outer perimeter and east-north-east gap through the inner. Datable to the fifth millennium BC this site belongs to the middle Neolithic of this region and as such predates the British sites by over a thousand years.

A similar and contemporary site at Kothingeichendorf-Landau is of a comparable size and lay-out to Viecht-Eching. Once more a double ditched enclosure contains traces of subsidiary circular structures showing as weaker anomalies on the geophysical data. Once more these are interpreted as palisade trenches with entrances appearing to coincide with causeways through the ditches **(fig 57)**. This site has four entrances which pass through both ditches and, like Mount Pleasant in Dorset or Tesetice Kyjovice, are arranged on the four cardinal points. This fascinating site appears to be part of a larger complex of conjoined twin-ditched enclosures spreading out towards the south-east with almost amoebic fission. Another double ditched enclosure is known at Gneiding-Oberpöring measuring some 75m in overall diameter with once again traces of weaker concentric anomalies in the interior. There are western and south-eastern coinciding entrances.

These sites are comparatively simple by some standards though the effects of erosion must be considered when making such broad observations. But more complex sites, bearing closer resemblance to Quenstedt, are also known. At Schmiedorf-Osterhofen two concentric palisades with a coinciding entrance to the south of east, encloses an area some 20m in diameter (Petrasch 1990). Around this ostensibly simple site is a triple ditched system some 75m in overall diameter **(fig 58)**. Entrances, once more coinciding, are located just north of west and to the east-south-east. There are also cardinally orientated

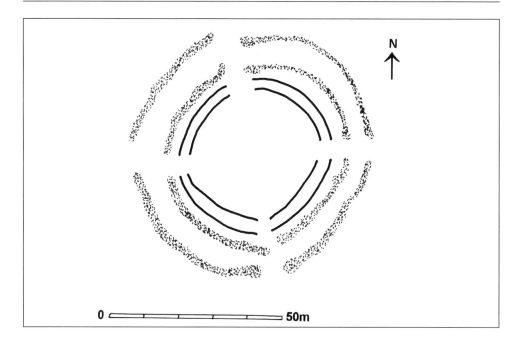

57   Plan of Kothingeichendorf (after the geophysical survey of Becker).

gaps in the outermost ditches to the north and south. An interesting feature at this site is that some of the ditch terminals appear to be linked thus closing off the intramural spaces. For example, the middle and inner ditches are tied together at the western entrance and outer and middle ditches are partially tied at the eastern entrance.

This closing of ditches is also paralleled at Unternberg-Künzing, the largest and most complex site to be investigated by the Bayerisches Landesamt für Denkmalpflege. Located within a large ditched enclosure, with tied entrances to the north-east, south-east, south-west and north-west lies a concentric oval complex 100m by 92m. The north-western entrance is swollen and slightly out-turned suggesting that the monument may have been grander at this point and that this may have been the principal of the four entrances **(fig 59)**. This gap also faces the gap through the outer enclosure. Within this tied ditch complex are five concentric palisade trenches; an outer pair enclosing a further three. Each of these palisades has entrances aligned on the ditch causeways and each exhibits a slight swelling towards the north-west. This uniformity suggests that the monument is a single-phased concept. The internal area enclosed is 34m by 24m.

A single palisaded site at Meisternthal is situated within the north-east sector of a kidney-shaped enclosure. This enclosure, itself with a palisaded perimeter, measures some 210m east-west by 140m north-south. The proven entrances appear to be in the eastern arc. The palisade circle itself is actually eliptical measuring 45m by 38m. It has two opposed entrances, due west and east and the main axis of the ellipse is north-south **(fig 60)**. Sightlines through the opposed entrances focus on the sunrises and sunsets at the equinoxes while by sighting from other points on the centre line, midsummer and

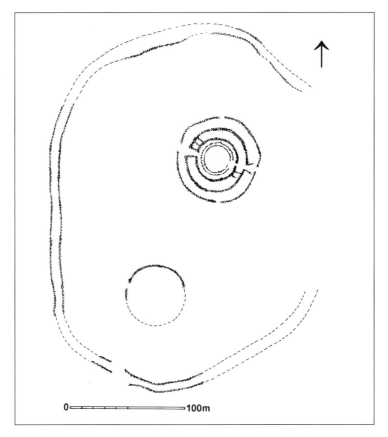

58 Plan of
Schmiedorf (after
the geophysical
survey of Becker).

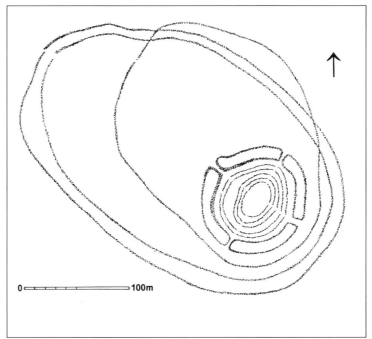

59 Plan of
Unternberg (after
the geophysical
survey of Becker).

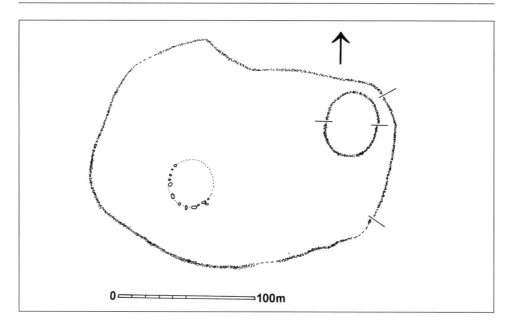

60   Plan of Miesternthal. The entrances are marked by lines (after the geophysical survey of
      Becker).

midwinter solar events can also be viewed. Apart from the morphology of the site, as well
as its fifth millennium date, the picture of cardinal and solar alignments is one with which
the British material has many parallels. The interpretation of the sites as 'Sonnentempel'
and 'Kalenderbauten' has a familiar ring.

Other sites in this peculiarly central European tradition were discussed by Petrasch in
the *Bericht der Romisch-Germanischen Kommission* for 1990. They have an unquestionable
similarity: outer enclosing multiple ditches with inner palisades and opposed multiple
entrances. Internal features appear to be absent though there are pits within the eastern
half of Friebritz 1 and a rectangular part posthole part bedding trench arrangement within
Bucany. Pits and postholes have been recognised in the geophysical surveys at other sites,
but the contemporaneity of these features with the main enclosing elements cannot be
demonstrated without excavation. Friebritz 1 is interesting in another respect. Between
the palisade and the inner ditch is a ring of 24 evenly spaced pairs of posts **(fig 61)**. They
resemble, albeit on a larger scale, the post pairs identified at Lugg in Co. Dublin and
Goldington in Bedfordshire. At the former site they were interpreted as trilithon
arrangements — more correctly trixylon, being made of wood — though clearly the
above-ground arrangement is one of conjecture.

As mentioned above, the entrances of the central European monuments are frequently
opposed, and often cardinally orientated. While the symmetry of the sites can find parallels
amongst the British corpus, the opposed entrances are less well known on this side of the
North Sea. Mount Pleasant is an obvious exception with cardinally orientated opposed
entrances through the timber circle, and some henges also have opposed entrances,

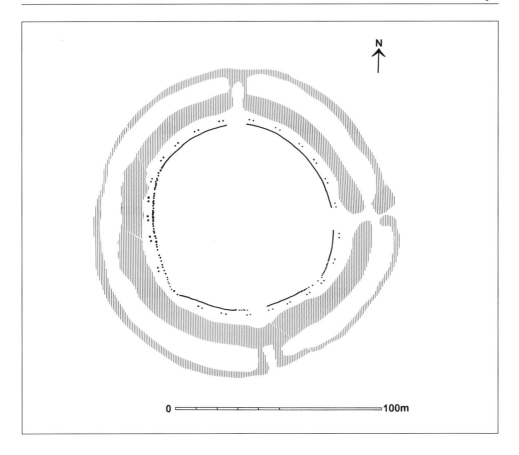

61   Friebritz 1 (after Petrasch).

though rarely more than two. The importance of these similarities is probably likely to be coincidence, however, bearing in mind the chronological and geographical separation of the two series.

The French material is limited at this point in time. However, French archaeology is currently dynamic and with round houses and Trevisker-like pottery currently being found in Normandy, a timber circle would not be unexpected. In the Vendée, at Terriers Avrillé, a double enclosure defined by two concentric circular bedding trenches was found associated with Beaker pottery (Benéteau *et al.* 1992). Two menhirs stood within the enclosure which had two entrances, one to the north-east and another to the west-north-west **(fig 62)**. The asymmetry of these entrances is more in keeping with British class II henges, but once again the parallel is probably coincidental rather than archaeologically significant. This bedding trench, describing an area 12.5m in diameter, held contiguous timbers, probably standing no more than shoulder high and a radiocarbon date of *c.*2100 BC demonstrates the contemporaneity of this site with the British material. This circle, interpreted as a sacred enclosure around the two standing stones, is so far unique in France but its wooden construction, its Beaker associations and its later Neolithic/earlier Bronze

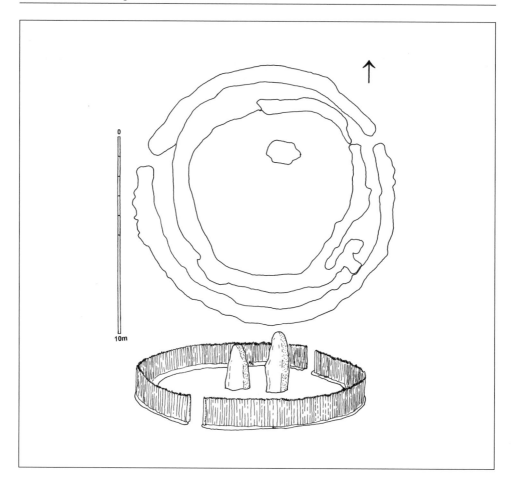

62   Terriers plan and reconstruction (after Benetau et al.).

Age radiocarbon date clearly suggest a certain affinity with the British material. It would, however, be dangerous to place too much significance on this superficial similarity until further sites are located and investigated.

In the Netherlands there are tantalising glimpses of a possible circle tradition. At Twisk, in North Holland, an oval of pits 8m by 6m in diameter was interpreted as a grain storage area and was C14-dated to about 1600 BC (Hristova 1984). It was associated with considerable quantities of flint waste which interestingly had a roughly cardinal distribution. The majority of the assemblage came from pits in the north and south of the site with lesser amounts to the east and west. Despite a superficial resemblance to timber ovals in Britain, there is, however, no evidence that the Twisk pits ever held posts.

At Ittersumerbroek on the outskirts of Zwolle in Overijssel, a bronze age settlement was excavated in advance of housing development. Two circular aragements of postholes were identified amongst the palimpsest of pits and postholes and these circles were subsequently interpreted as solar calendars. These circles measured 11m in diameter and

63   Zwolle, the south-west circle (courtesy of Jan de Jong).

comprised 14 postholes. The excavators admitted that the groundplan of each circle individually is not particularly convincing, but taken together, the groundplans and dimensions of the two circles are so similar that they are unlikely to be coincidental **(fig 63)**. Indeed the two circles can be superimposed and of the 14 postholes in each circle, nine overlap while of the others there is less than 0.3m separation (de Jong & Wevers, 1994: de Jong 1998). Both circles have a radially set pair of postholes in the east. This radial pairing, though not necessarily cardinally set, can be matched at Goldington and Cairnpapple. Both circles had a putative entrance, marked by a wider gap, towards the south and their geometry is remarkably similar.

The centre point to the radial pair of postholes is aligned due east on the equinox, or more correctly a point midway between midsummer and midwinter sunrise. To the south-east of each circle lies an outlying post which marks an orientation to the midwinter sunset. A line north from this outlying posthole passing through the eastern post could be extended northwards to form an isosceles triangle with a line north-west from the centre. This centre to north-east sightline is orientated on the midsummer sunrise. Unfortunately there are no posts in this position associated with either circle: the hypothetical position lay outside the excavated area of the southern circle and within an area of later disturbance with regard to the northern. Largely because of a perceived lack of circular monuments in the Netherlands at this time, these circles have not gained universal acceptance amongst Dutch archaeologists. But de Jong has argued a convincing case for there being little chance of coincidence in their design. Had they been found in Britain, there would have been much more comparative data and their validity would have been far more acceptable.

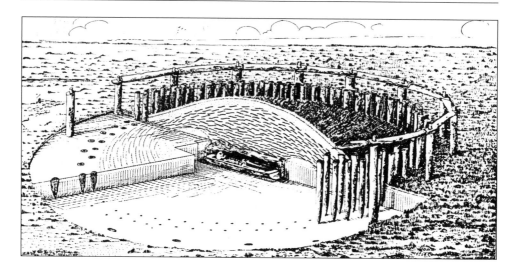

64   van Giffen's reconstruction of Wessinghuizen.

Timber circles at round barrow sites are far more common in the Netherlands and, due to the excellent survival that the sands of the country afford, it is often possible to demonstrate that the posts projected through the mounds. At Wessinghuizen near Groningen, for example, a double palisade of posts encircled the outer limits of a turf mound (van Giffen 1930). Beyond this was a third post-setting, an encircling ring of 16 evenly-spaced posts which van Giffen reconstructed as having lintels fixed with mortice and tenon joints **(fig 64)**. The reconstruction has no basis in fact. There is no archaeological proof for this reconstruction, often regarded as fanciful. But van Giffen looked towards Britain for his parallels. Woodhenge had recently been published and the Cunnington's suggestion that Woodhenge may have been lintelled like its lithic neighbour was an attractive one. At Langedeif in Friesland and Noordische Veld in Drenthe substantial well-spaced posts also projected through the mound but van Giffen's reconstructions here were far less adventurous.

Van Giffen (1930; 1938) published some 20 'Palissadenheuvels' or palisaded mounds in the Netherlands the groundplans of which can be paralleled in Britain. Both palisades, possibly acting as retaining fences, as well as free-standing circles are present and occasionally cardinal orientations can be identified. There are east and west entrances at Uddel and a post-pairing at the south at Langedijk. At other sites, the evenly spaced nature of the posts makes orientation, if present at all, difficult to identify.

Free-standing post circles, the posts also penetrating through the mound, were excavated by Glasbergen (1954) in the decade after the war at the cemetery of Toterfout/Halve Mijl in North Brabant **(fig 65)**. The post circle at Barrow 15 has an inturned entrance towards the east and there is also a flattening of the multiple circled barrow 19 in this direction. Barrow 24 also has a gap to the east through its double palisade. But Glasbergen, in his wide-ranging study, concluded that there was little consistency in the orientation of entrances. At Barrow 75 **(fig 66)**, orientated to the south-

65   Reconstructed post-circle barrow in the Toterfout/Halve Mijl cemetery, Brabant.

east, was a timber avenue some 35m long. Terminating in a post to the south-east and a multiple post circle to the north-west, the site resembles the double stone rows of Dartmoor **(colour plate 8)** rather than the British post avenues associated with insular timber circles.

In a raised bog at Bargeroosterveld in the provice of Drenthe, Waterbolk and van Zeist (1961) published what could only be interpreted as a Bronze Age sanctuary or temple **(fig 67)**. Here, surrounded by a circular bank of rounded stones, a square setting of posts and planks was located with roughly east-west and north-south axes. At this fascinating site, the reconstruction is hardly in doubt since the wood survived in the waterlogged conditions of the bog. Pegged into two broad planks were four uprights which supported two lintels. Two other lintels joined the ends of the plank-set lines. These lintels were fitted using mortice and tenon joints and the ends of the lintels were curved upwards, resembling, though not necessarily representative of, cattle horns. Two larger and perhaps lower, posts stood in the centre of the south-west and north-east sides but their functions are not understood. The reconstruction of this site has a peculiarly oriental look with its slender wooden uprights and its projecting upturned lintel terminals. Unfortunately this site is still unique in western European archaeology. It is unknown to what extent, if at all, it can be linked to the circle tradition. Its middle Bronze Age radiocarbon date of *c.* 1400-1050 BC clearly places it at the end of the British circle-building sequence **(colour plate 9)**.

The European material, particularly that from the Netherlands, clearly indicates that there are similarities between timber circles in Britain and in Europe. What is less certain

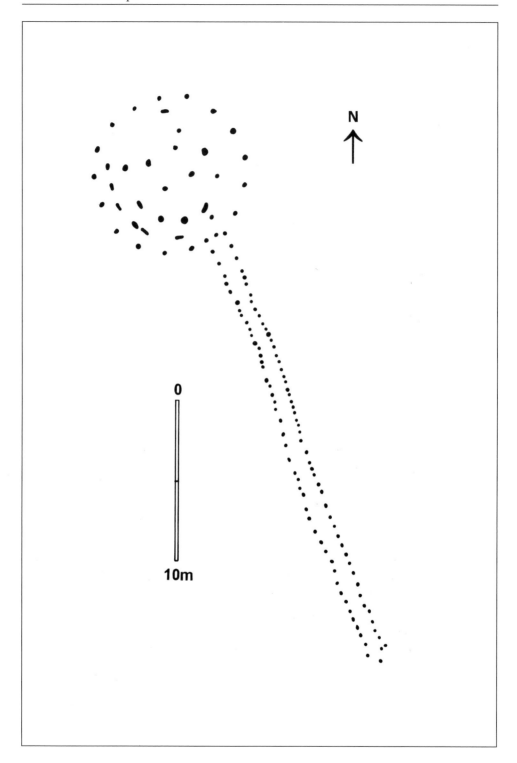

66   Plan of Barrow 75 in the Toterfout/Halve Mijl cemetery, Brabant (after Glasbergen).

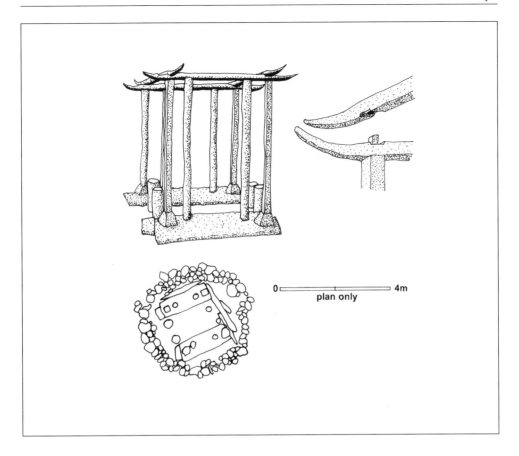

67   *Bargeroosterveld, Drenthe. Reconstruction, plan and detail of the timber temple (after
      Waterbolk & van Zeist). Reconstruction and detail not to scale.*

is the relationship between the different groups. The German material, for example, has
fundamentally different architecture and it dates to over a millennium earlier than the
British and Irish material. There are, nevertheless, certain similarities, in particular the
cardinal and solar orientations. This is perhaps less important than it might appear at face-
value. In agrarian societies where life itself depended on the returning seasons and the
rebirth of the vernal sun, it is natural that the solar orb be venerated and observed. Its
rising places on the horizon at certain important times of the year — sowing, harvest and
its turning points at mid-summer and winter — would be well known and the success of
the year's harvest would in part depend on its benevolence. Thus solar observation is
common to most agrarian societies and is capable of independent development. What
links the Continental and insular traditions therefore is the sun, the materials from which
they were built and the agrarian societies which built them. Common traditions beyond
the most general probably do not need to be sought.

5 The functions of timber circles

The functions performed by these timber circles are difficult to determine. Their layouts, their monumentality, their investment in human resources, all testify to the deep convictions held by their builders, but the sounds, smells and mysticism doubtless once associated with these wooden temples have all long since perished. Archaeoastronomers and mathematicians have claimed numerous stellar orientations for megalithic sites and formulated complex calendrical functions for rings of stone or timber (see Burl 1983; Ruggles 1998; Ruggles & Whittle (eds) 1981 for discussions). But whilst the arguments for and against these calculations are beyond the critical capabilities of the present writer it must be remembered that proving sites *could* have been used in this way does not prove that they *were*. Furthermore, if these sites were complex calendars and observatories then they suggest a level of numeracy amongst the prehistoric population far in excess of that which has hitherto been imagined and predating the presocratic mathematics of Pythagoras by many centuries.

Nevertheless, timber circles consist, at their simplest, of formal predetermined arrangements of substantial wooden uprights. Moreover, the actual monument may have been far more complex than the ground plans suggest. Even at their simplest, at face or ground plan value, timber circles represent monumental constructions which, to their architects and builders, would have had prescribed functions, forms dictated by tradition and predetermined points and modes of access and egress. The building of these temples would have served specifically identified ritual or religious needs. The practice of these rituals would have been essential in preserving the *status quo*, maintaining society's ordering and ensuring the continuity of life-systems. It is those actual rituals which, after three millennia, largely escape us. Nevertheless, some hints remain.

On the other hand, the cardinal (and therefore probably solar) orientation of some entrances and/or other architectural features can certainly be demonstrated. For example, at Sarn-y-bryn-caled, the entrance was marked by wider and taller posts **(fig 68)** and was orientated more or less due south given the constraints of the Severn valley's horizons. At Caebetin, in an upland location within the Severn Valley, larger diameter posts were situated in the east and west while a triangular stone was set upright in the south. At Litton Cheney, the entrance was more or less due east and the avenues of Ogden Down, Stonehenge and Durrington Walls North all approach their circles from the south. At Mount Pleasant, the wider aisles are more or less cardinally orientated and at Stonehenge the frequently ignored southern entrance through the bank and ditch must also be remembered. At Woodhenge **(fig 69)** an interest in the cardinal points can also be

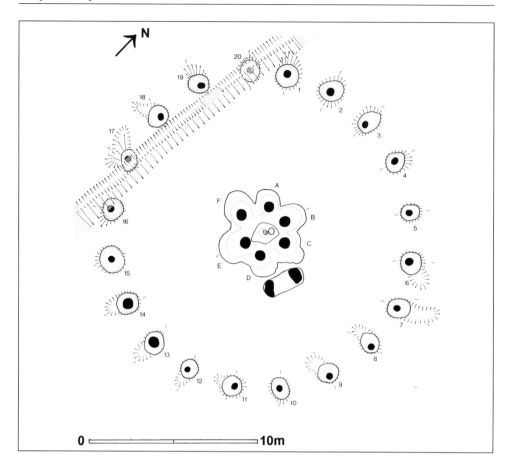

68   *Plan of the timber circle at Sarn-y-bryn-caled, Powys (drawn by Brian Williams, ©CPAT).*

demonstrated with special deposits being placed in postholes to the north and south of the central point and the majority of the ceramic finds seem to have been derived from the old ground surface below the southern and, to a lesser extent, western arcs of the bank. At Balfarg, there is also a southern causeway through the ditch and the majority of ceramic finds come from the southern and south-eastern arcs of the circle.

Once one of the site's cardinal points has been established, most easily south, by observing the midday winter sun, the other points may be calculated and other orientations can be deduced. Burl (1991) has convincingly described the solar alignments at Woodhenge where very narrow windows exist between posts to allow orientations on the midwinter and midsummer sunrises (**colour plate 10**). Dorchester 3 is an ovoid with its apex towards the south-east, the direction of the midwinter sunrise, and the timber circles at Newgrange and Durrington Walls South also share a similar orientation. At the Newgrange passage grave there lies above the entrance to the tomb a small aperture with decorated lintel known as the Newgrange roof-box (**colour plate 11**). This letterbox-like opening was precisely aligned to allow the rays of the rising midwinter sun to penetrate

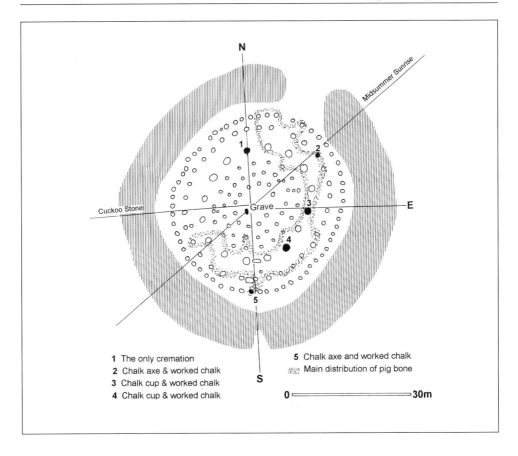

N

Midsummer Sunrise

1

2

Cuckoo Stone

Grave

3

E

4

5

S

1 The only cremation
2 Chalk axe & worked chalk
3 Chalk cup & worked chalk
4 Chalk cup & worked chalk

5 Chalk axe and worked chalk
Main distribution of pig bone

0 ⟞━━━━━━━━━━━⟝ 30m

69   *Deposition patterns at Woodhenge (based on plans by Burl and Pollard).*

the innermost recesses of the chamber, the heart of the tomb. At Stonehenge, the trilithons of the inner horseshoe, rise in height towards the central setting and the midwinter sunset is framed in the gap between the two uprights: a gap which appears to have narrowed towards its base.

Given these rare survivals, timber circles can only pose the question of what wooden architectural and astronomical devices may have survived above ground level to have similarly illuminated the inner sanctum or sancta at specific solar events. Certainly, where it can be demonstrated, solar observation (cardinal and eastern orientations) seems to be a common interest.

Solar orientations have been extrapolated for the similar Dutch sites. At Zwolle (de Jong & Wevers 1994: de Jong 1998), there is an eastern orientation as well as alignments with posts marking the midwinter and midsummer sunrise (**fig 70**). In the southern Netherlands, many of the wooden circle barrows are orientated due east, a cardinal and equinoctial focus, and are situated in places such as by water, where flat horizons can be easily obtained (inf Willem Beex). In Germany cardinal orientations are again visible and at Miesternthal, two opposed entrances in a north-south orientated elipse, have possible

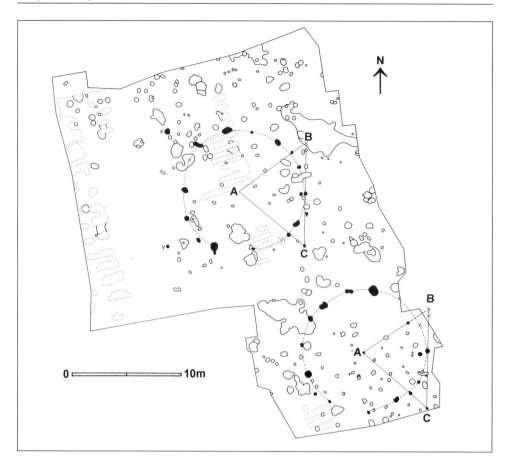

70   *Plan of the postulated timber circles at Zwolle Ittersumerbroek A-B and A-C are sightlines on the midsummer and midwinter sunrises respectively (courtesy of Jan de Jong).*

equinoctial orientations (Becker 1996).

If cardinal, lunar or solar orientations are accepted then the circles may be deemed to also have had a calendrical function in that the positions of the solar body at specific recurring intervals can be demonstrated and observed. The complexity of this calendar, however, remains to be demonstrated. There has over the last two decades been an attempt by some scholars to demonstrate both the ability of prehistoric astronomers to locate often obscure celestial bodies through precise geometry and (at least to a humble archaeologist) an overwhelming astronomical knowledge. This deduction has, however, often been at the expense of the natural and archaeological data and thus stars may have been mis-sited, or stones, dislocated and no longer *in situ*, may have been employed in the sightlines. This criticism is not to deny the existence of celestial observations in the Neolithic and Bronze Age, however, but is designed more as an exercise of caution since, logically, it would be possible to orientate a circle, with a circumference of 360 degrees, on any, or indeed all, celestial events. However, there is an increasing body of evidence to suggest that the sun and moon in particular were observed at specific times of the year and this has been demonstrated at numerous sites of this period in Britain by the works of more discerning scholars such as Aubrey Burl, Clive Ruggles and John Barnatt. As has already been mentioned, in the Netherlands, equinoctial orientations seem to have been preferred while at Zwolle Ittersumerbroek orientations could be demonstrated for the sunrises on 21 March, June, September and December as well as early May, later to become the Celtic feast of Beltane and the Spring festival.

Other interpretations are, needless to say, occasionally proposed. For example Derrick Lees (1984) has calculated a complex calendrical role for the Sanctuary based on alternate years of 365 and 366 days involving an abacus-like use of the outer and inner stone circles combined with lunar observation. He calculates that the alignments present at the site and embodied in his argument would only have a 1 in 100 chance of being fortuitous. As mentioned above, this is one theory which, if correct, suggests a level of numeracy amongst the prehistoric population not previously envisaged.

Whilst burials occur at some timber circles, it does not appear appropriate to label them as burial sites. Burials are found around and inside churches but to call a church a burial site is to ignore its other functions: worship, marriage, baptism and the wider social roles within the community. Indeed, few timber circles have a primary association with burial. For example the central child sacrifice at Woodhenge need not be stratigraphically primary and at Sarn-y-bryn-caled the central cremation was certainly stratigraphically secondary to the inner circle; the burial pit having been dug through the fill of the inner postholes. At both sites, burial is undoubtedly important but need have been neither one of the initial ceremonies nor indeed the primary function of the monument. Elsewhere, burial is clearly secondary. For example Beaker and Food Vessel burials were made at Balfarg and North Mains perhaps as many as 400 years after the construction of the primary timber monuments. At Dorchester 3, cremation burials were deposited in the tops of the postholes after the timber circle had been dismantled and at Oddendale the timber circle was replaced by a Bronze Age ring cairn with associated cremations. At Brenig 44, the timber circle was later covered by a bank around the ring cairn and with Bronze Age cremations being deposited late in the site's history (**fig 71**). At Stonehenge, burials were placed in the tops of the Aubrey holes, particularly those close to the southern entrance, prior to their final filling and almost as a final gesture. Especially important burials were also placed in the ditch terminals at both entrances.

Most notably at the large Wessex henges, where the chalky soil is conducive to the survival of faunal remains, there appears to be evidence for feasting. This would seem to have taken place at Durrington Walls, Mount Pleasant, Marden and Woodhenge and is represented by the large quantities of immature or young adult pig bones recovered from the excavations at these sites. The pig is generally regarded as a feasting animal and its importance in later Celtic society again points at the possible origins of much of what we regard as Celtic religion. The Wessex sites benefit greatly from their geology and while the soils of northern and upland sites are rarely conducive to the survival of faunal remains, note may also be made at this point that fragments of cremated pig bones were associated with the Sarn-y-bryn-caled burials and pig fats have been recovered from Grooved Ware pottery in the Welsh Marches. The picture is not a simple one, however. The faunal

71   *Reconstruction of the timber circle and ring cairn at Brenig 44, Denbighshire (courtesy of Frances Lynch).*

preponderances differ dramatically at Durrington Walls in favour of pigs at the Southern and cattle at the Northern Circles, and sheep bones have also been recovered in significant quantities from the Sanctuary and Woodhenge. But feasting is again unlikely to be the primary function of these monuments, rather an important part of elaborate rituals and ceremonies which have otherwise left little evidence in the archaeological record.

Furthermore, in view of the depositional differences at the two Durrington Walls circles, it may be that differing rituals were undertaken at superficially similar sites. A word of caution may also be offered at this point and that is that it is dangerous to infer too much from limited data. The animal bones at these sites generally come from the upper fills of the postholes and are therefore secondary and potentially late in the sites' histories. They may even have found their way there after the sites' demise, just as did the Iron Age bronze-working at Sarn-y-bryn-caled, and one is reminded of the trappings of modern society such as old bicycles, bottles, cans and, most of all, supermarket trolleys which frequently end up not-so-ritually deposited in redundant buildings.

Despite this pessimistic, but probably realistic, caution, ritually charged material was certainly deposited at many timber circles. Colin Richards and Julian Thomas (1984) have argued convincingly for the structured deposition of Grooved Ware at Durrington Walls. Here they identified a Grooved Ware hierarchy with undecorated vessels at the lower end and highly decorated pots at the upper. According to their scheme lower levels of Grooved Ware came from the Northern Circle while sherds with richer decoration came from the Southern Circle, the Midden and the Platform. These sherds almost certainly represent deliberate deposition rather than casual disposal and were frequently found decoration uppermost. It seems we must envisage a practice or ritual in which it was important to place particular types of ceramics at specific points within the structure.

Burl (1991) has also demonstrated a similar practice of specific deposition within the timber rings of Woodhenge but here the deposits were much more varied. For example, the only cremation lies due north of centre in the C ring. Also in the C ring, a chalk cup and other worked chalk come from due east of centre and also on the midwinter sunrise. A chalk axe and worked chalk were deposited due south of centre as well as on the midsummer sunrise in the A and B rings respectively. These deposits were the only finds from low in the post-holes and are restricted to the outer three rings as were the overwhelming majority of pig bones from the site (Pollard 1992). These artefacts probably represent deliberate depositions and it is not inconceivable that the posts were themselves marked in some way to reinforce the significance of their orientations. It has also been noted that the majority of the pottery was recovered from pre-henge contexts and once more there are distinct groupings from the southern arc and from due west of centre returning us to the cardinal orientations outlined above.

Pollard (1992) further argues for a broadly similar pattern of deposition at the Sanctuary with an emphasis on the eastern quadrant while at Balfarg, pottery predominates in the postholes of the southern and western arc of circle A, close to and south of the entrance. The postholes of the north and east were devoid of ceramic finds. Even the unstratified flint focused on the post ring as though it was derived from the plough-truncated upper fills of the post sockets and thus recalls the Grooved Ware at Durrington Walls. At Charnham Lane, Hungerford the only finds, two fragments of Aldbourne cup, were found in posthole 5007, due south of centre and at Lawford, a concentration of Grooved Ware was found on the inner edge of the ditch at the north of the site. The upper levels of the posthole fills at Knowth (**colour plate 12**) had deliberate Grooved Ware deposits while at Dorchester 3 all the pottery came from postholes in the eastern arc while flint was recovered from the south-western arc. It may be straining the evidence to read too much into this dichotomy of deposition in view of the general paucity of finds from this site but nevertheless it appears to be another site where intentional deposition has taken place: deliberately deposited material placed at strategic and predetermined points within the monument.

It is difficult, virtually impossible, to know exactly what forms the rituals took at these religious sites. We have determined that they involved the structured deposition of artefacts and food remains at specific locales within the monument. We have seen that there was a preoccupation with cardinal and calendrical orientations which imply the observation of at least the solar orb if not the lunar also. These are detectable facets of the rituals manifested in the tangible remains preserved in the archaeological record. But religions also involve other more esoteric rituals which will have less of a permanent effect on the physical remains.

One such ritual is that of procession; an element common to many religions or ritualistic practices. Procession involves the ordered assembly of individuals approaching or leaving the focal site in a prescribed and predetermined fashion. Doubtless such approaches were also part of the rituals performed at timber circles.

The West Kennet Avenue (**fig 72**), marked by pairs of opposed fat and thin stones, runs between Avebury and the Sanctuary on Overton Hill. This monument must be the most concrete of evidence for processions in British Prehistory linking as it does two major religious *loci*, being (unlike cursus monuments) open-ended (thus allowing through

72   *The West Kennet avenue with opposed fat and thin stones (courtesy of Aubrey Burl).*

passage), and being wide enough to accommodate people, animals and the trappings of ceremony. The Stonehenge Avenue leading from (or to) the River Avon to the north-east entrance of Stonehenge via a circuitous route similarly begs interpretation as a formal approach to the monument, wide enough to channel people up to the henge but too narrow to permit a massive throng. It leads through an entrance gap in the sarsen ring marked by a slightly wider space, and the orientation continues through the bluestone circle towards the back of the sarsen horseshoe and the window for the midwinter sunset formed by the tallest and central sarsen trilithon.

The timber avenues at Durrington Walls, Lugg, Poole, Ogden Down and Stonehenge 1, leading at this site from the southern entrance, further support the more general or widespread idea of formalised approach to other monuments of the period. At Durrington Walls, and Stonehenge I where there are also screens associated with the avenues, there is the suggestion that there was an attempt to further formalise the avenue by preventing visual contact with the site from any but the correct and predetermined approach.

Even within sites without apparent avenues, procession or formalised entry may be inferred by the arrangement of posts or by the orientation of circles within their immediate environments. For example at Bleasdale, assuming the contemporaneity of the timber circle and the outer palisade, the palisade opens to the south-south-west while the timber circle has an eastern entrance marked by a short splayed avenue leading almost up to the surrounding palisade (**fig 73**). Participants in the ritual at this site would not have been able to have walked directly from the entrance of the palisade to the entrance of the timber circle but would have had to have taken a circuitous route. Similarly at Sarn-y-bryn-caled the outer circle had its entrance to the south while the inner circle appears to have opened to the west, or possibly the east (**fig 74**) again suggesting an attempt to avoid

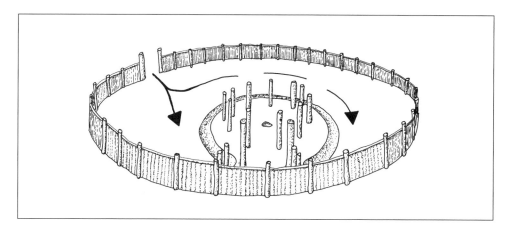

73 *Reconstruction of the Bleasdale circle, Lancashire (after Gibson) with possible routes of entry marked.*

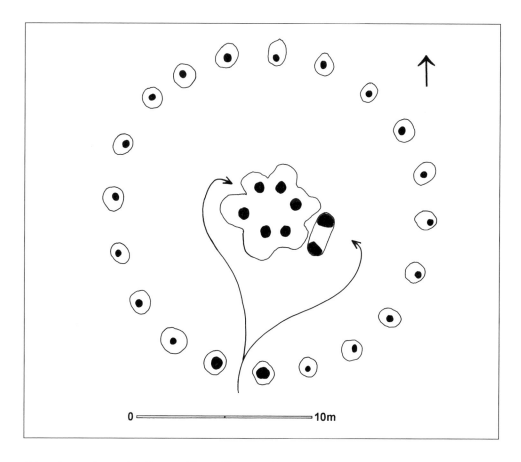

74 *Sarn-y-bryn-caled, Powys with possible routes of entry to the inner circle. A wider gravel causeway indicated a possible entrance to the west while the two-post structure in the east may be a porch.*

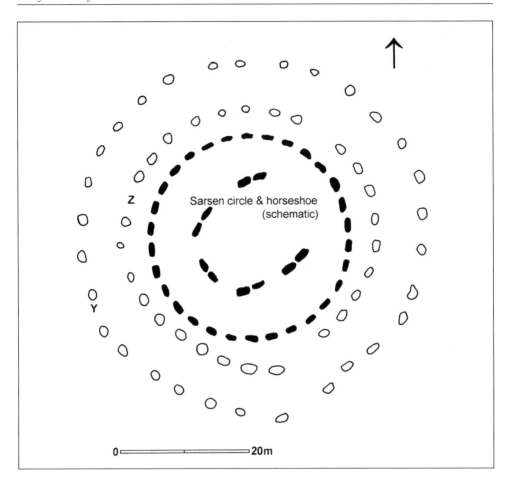

Sarsen circle & horseshoe
(schematic)

75   *The Y & Z holes at Stonehenge with the sarsens added for reference. Note the irregularity of the circles to the south-east (after Cleal et al.).*

a direct approach. Therefore at both Bleasdale and Sarn-y-bryn-caled it is possible to envisage access to the innermost part of the site being deliberately indirect and also, by the same token, the inner sanctum being obscured when viewed from the main entrance. This may also explain the spiralling nature of the Y and Z stone-holes at Stonehenge (**fig 75**). These holes do not form perfect concentric circles but rather spiral in towards the presumed southern entrance to the innermost phase 1 monument perhaps leading celebrants around the monument, to or from a possible entrance/exit opposite the southern ditch causeway.

One is immediately reminded of the frieze of the Parthenon on the Athenian Acropolis. This frieze celebrates the Panathenaic procession from the sanctuary, and one time rival of Athens, at Eleusis to the temple of Athena on the Acropolis and took a new cloak or *peplos* to the olive wood cult statue in the temple. It travelled down the Sacred Way. This road had been the prescribed route, the avenue, for centuries and even commanded its own

76   *Section of the Parthenon frieze among the Elgin Marbles in the British Museum. The
sculptures illustrate a religious procession in all its stages.*

gateway through the Athenian town walls, a gateway open only during the Panathenaic
festivals. The procession passed through this gate, through the Agora and entered the
Acropolis from the west through the great and imposing Propyleion. The temple of
Athena, like all Greek temples, opened to the east but the procession entered the precinct
from the west and so were only able to enter the temple by perambulating the interior of
the city sanctuary. The sculptures on the frieze, representing the celebrants and their
sacrifices, also indicate the growing solemnity of the event. At the western, more distant,
end the people are inattentive and the animals are straining and poorly controlled. At the
eastern, or proximal end, the procession is more restrained, more respectful, the animals
more controlled as the procession approaches the deity (**fig 76**). At the height of Athens'
power, and after the coffers of the Delian League had financed the Periclean building
programme on the Acropolis, the procession would have wound its way round the
Parthenon before ultimately approaching the Erectheion wherein lay the olive wood cult
statue of Athena. It was a time for Athens' glory to be observed: for the Parthenon — a
show-piece and not a temple — to be admired and for Athenian achievement to be
celebrated. Processions rarely have a single objective.

   The lack of direct access to the interior of timber circles has also been recently
demonstrated by Pollard (1992) for Mount Pleasant site IV and the Sanctuary. At the
former site, obstructions within the corridors formed by the concentric arrangements
effectively created a circular maze with entry to the *sanctum sanctorum* being controlled and
predetermined (**fig 77**). However, this presupposes that the uprights were linked by
horizontals, fencing or perhaps screening, to close the gaps between them except in the

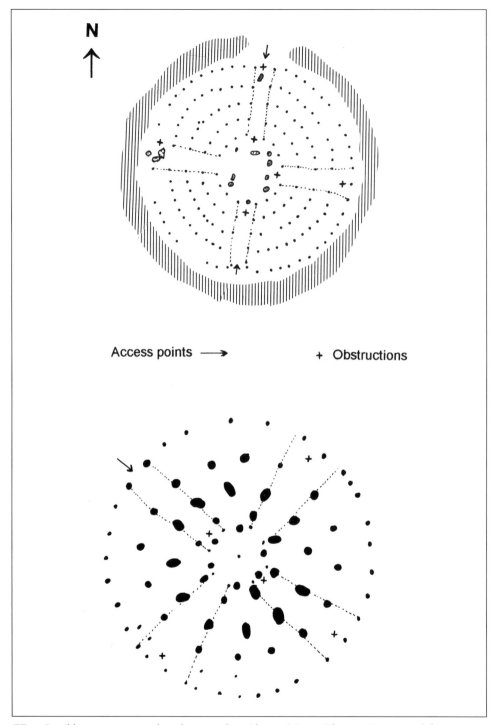

77   *Possible access routes and predetermined corridors at Mount Pleasant (upper) and the*
      Sanctuary (after Pollard).

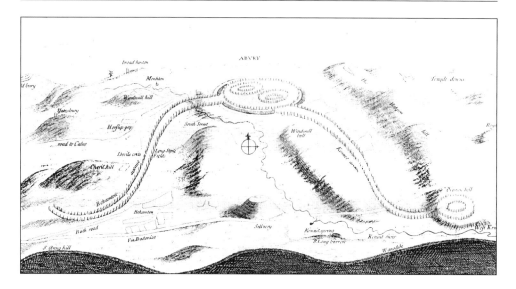

78   *Stukeley's plan of avenues at Avebury. Despite the obvious artistic licence avenues such as this are our strongest evidence for prehistoric processions.*

instances where entrances were designed. At Woodhenge, snail shells from *Lymnaea peregra*, *Planorbis leucostoma* and *Succinea pfeifferi* were recovered from the ditch. These species are generally associated with fresh water habitats yet Woodhenge is on the dry chalkland overlooking the Avon. It was therefore suggested that these wetland species were brought to the site in reeds or river mud. The reeds may well have been used for thatching. But reeds may also have been woven into matting or mud may have been plastered onto wattling so that solid screens between the uprights may well have existed at this site too. At Sarn-y-bryn-caled, the upper fills of the posthole weathering cones had a high clayey fraction and clay had been burnt when the inner circle had burnt down suggesting again the presence of wattle and daub between the uprights, certainly of the inner circle if less certainly the outer.

Screens or barriers between the uprights have also been suggested by the respective excavators at the outer ring of Machrie Moor I and North Mains where carbonised planking was recovered. If the interpretations are correct, then this hypothesis has still greater significance. At an increasing number of sites there seems to be a very real attempt to deny visual access to the interior of circles and henges. The screens at Durrington Walls have already been described and serve to restrict visual access into the monument; only from the avenue can a full view of the entrance be obtained. For $1\frac{1}{2}$ miles (2.4km), the West Kennet Avenue at Avebury (**fig 78**) leads more or less directly northwards to Avebury's southern entrance. However, the final 400m or so sees a swing westwards, away from the entrance. Finally it then turns dramatically back to lead directly towards the entrance in its last 100m. It is only in this last 100m that a full view of Avebury's southern entrance is obtained and the approachers would have been faced with the massive chalk banks and, immediately inside, Avebury's two largest stones. Moreover, these large stones do not flank the entrance but rather the western of the pair is central to the causeway and the eastern monolith lies in line with the eastern ditch terminal (**colour plate 13**). The positioning of these stones further serves to obscure the interior of the henge when viewed from the avenue and thus they preserve the mystery until its ultimate but inevitable revelation.

Similarly the curved nature of the Stonehenge avenue ensured that the circle entrance was only visible for the final part of the uphill journey from the Avon. At the circle itself, the positioning of the irregular bluestone circle within the sarsen ring effectively blocked the gaps between the outer uprights and obscured vision into the interior. Indeed the very banks of henge monuments themselves may be seen as devices to prevent vision into the interiors of the enclosures. Henge banks have been variously interpreted as barriers and viewing platforms. If the latter then the spectators would still be kept at a respectful distance from the proceedings by the enormous internal ditch. But if a viewing platform, then why were the banks not flat-topped and furthermore why is the bank to the east of the northern entrance at Avebury still unfinished? Henge banks are often increased in height at their entrances, again suggesting an attempt to conceal the interior, an extra obstacle at the point of greatest contact. The possibility of postholes being cut into or through the bank in Cutting 44 at Stonehenge (Cleal *et al.* 1995) may also argue in favour of a palisade having originally topped the bank, perhaps further acting as a barrier to obscure the interior from the less privileged or the uninitiated.

This leads us to consider the whole concept of exclusion and whether timber circles were open to all members of the society or whether they were the preserves of the few. Where the evidence allows, there appears to be a distinct pattern suggesting an element of exclusion at many ritual sites of the period. As mentioned above with regard to henges, banks keep the masses out as well as the privileged in and the enlarged entrances at many henges would convey grandeur to the approaching participants as well as acting as a physical barrier. Portal posts in some henge entrances, for example at Gorsey Bigbury in Somerset (**fig 79**) may even have supported gate structures to further restrict access (ApSimon *et al.* 1976). These combined features might therefore suggest that at least some of the rites within henges may have been accessible only to a qualified few with right of entry to the interior. Even allowing for popular access to the tops of the banks, eager spectators here would still have been denied physical access by the internal ditch. Even then, ceremonies within the timber circles in henges may still have been secretive.

Enclosure itself defines space and creates a difference between the area within and the area without. It follows that a similar very real distinction would have existed between the *people* within and without also, even if this distinction was only relevant during the currency of the festivals. Thus the differences noted above in the orientation of enclosure entrances and the entrances of the timber circles they contain may be a further device designed to create a deliberate act of exclusion. At Stonehenge itself, in its final complex phase, there is no evidence for any blocking between the uprights of the outer sarsen circle. Nevertheless the ceremonies which took place within the inner trilithon horseshoe would have been largely concealed to an audience situated outside the enclosure by the inner bluestone circle. Despite the complex geometry of the monument, only really visible in plan and from the air, the view from the ground would have been one of internal clutter.

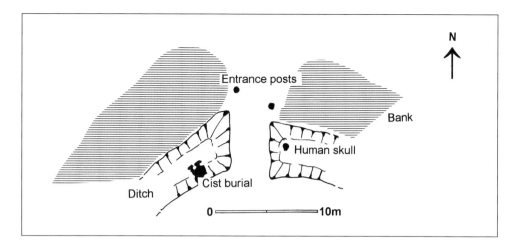

79   *The entrance to the henge at Gorsey Bigbury, Somerset with ritually charged deposits of human skeletal material at the ditch terminals (after Burl).*

Taking the physical barriers discussed above with regard to procession, the evidence for planking and daub noted at some sites such as Machrie Moor and North Mains, and the very real attempt to define specific entrances at others, then it seems almost certain that the goings on inside circles were by and large invisible to those outside and therefore restricted to an elite — probably a priesthood. From this a multi-tiered society may be envisaged, certainly within a religious context: those who were excluded, those who were permitted and those who controlled access.

As has been mentioned and as will be discussed again, Stonehenge originally housed a multiple timber circle within the interior, linked to the southern entrance by an avenue, and ultimately replaced by the grand stone design we see today. The exact form of this timber circle is difficult to reconstruct since the postholes were excavated at different times, by different people and to differing standards. Furthermore, subsequent rebuilding has doubtless destroyed the evidence for many others.

Burl (1987) originally envisaged a double circle at Stonehenge which he interpreted as a charnel house, where human corpses were left to decay, where the dead were left to corrupt and, by this process of decay, were enabled to complete their journey to the otherworld aided by the defleshing agencies of carrion birds, carnivorous insects and gnawing rodents. The evidence for the exposure and defleshing of corpses in the Neolithic is strong and mortuary structures have been interpreted at Balfarg **(fig 80)** and Ballynahatty **(fig 81)**. Some circles may well have involved this rite of passage with the inedible parts of animals, notably their skulls, accompanying the human dead. The evidence is not, however, conclusive. We have no proof that the 'divers animal' remains recorded in antiquarian excavations at Stonehenge are in any way specific, nor are we certain that they date to the timber phase any more than the stone. Animal remains at other timber circles are interpreted as the remains of feasts and not as totemic offerings, though, quite why the debris from feasts and banquets should be left lying around the

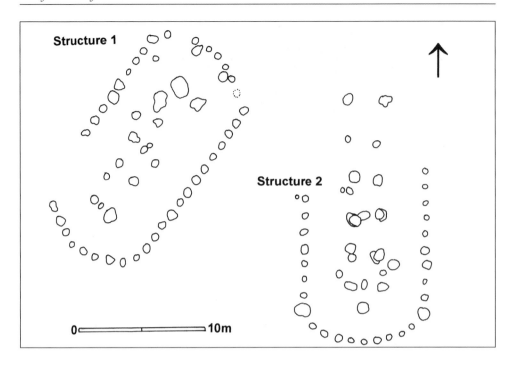

80   Two structures discovered at Balfarg, Fife and interpreted as enclosed mortuary structures with exposure platforms represented by the internal postholes (after Barclay).

interior is a question which is rarely addressed. While we can assume that the early antiquaries could recognise ox skulls, we have no reason to believe that any attention would be paid to other, less recognisable, skulls or skull fragments. We also have no idea as to the authenticity of 'reported' findings, to what extent they have been augmented by the very thrill of having excavated in such a monument, and, of course, we have no idea of the archaeological context of such reported finds. It is not suggested here that the early reportings ought to be ignored altogether, but that in such cases strict caution ought to be applied and that one should not place too much reliance on them.

The mortuary house hypothesis is also attractive but unproven. Human remains at timber circles, even in areas where bone would be expected to survive, are rare. While it may be argued that the defleshed bones may have been taken off for burial elsewhere, nevertheless one might expect to find some smaller bones, for example from the hands and feet, which might have fallen off during the natural process of decay and have been scattered by the activities of the fauna attracted to the macabre feast. Instead we find that burial tends to be secondary and often once the circle has ceased to function in its original form. The cremation deposits in the upper levels of former postholes at Stonehenge (Aubrey Holes), Dorchester 3 and the secondary burials at Balfarg and North Mains have already been mentioned in this context. In short there is no evidence for a preoccupation with death or with a primary sepulchral intention at any timber circle.

However, two particularly macabre deposits may be mentioned at this point. The first

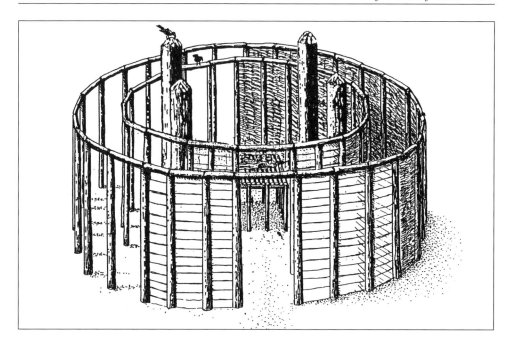

81   Reconstruction of the Ballynahatty timber circle with exposure platforms represented by the internal four-post setting. The reconstruction bears a striking resemblance to that proposed for Sarn-y-bryn-caled, a coincidence which the present writer finds comforting (courtesy of Barrie Hartwell).

burial at Sarn-y-bryn-caled was secondary to the construction of the circle since the burial pit was partly dug through the fillings of the postholes of the inner circle. This burial, of a young but mature adult of unknown sex, contained amongst the bones, the burnt remains of four Conygar type flint arrowheads **(fig 82** and **colour plate 14)**. These early Bronze Age arrowheads frequently accompany burials and are noted for the high quality of the workmanship (Green 1980). By gradually chipping and flaking the flint, master craftsmen were able to form elegant points, with long slender barbs and an equally well-fashioned tang for fixing the head to its shaft. The points were needle sharp and the edges like razors. Some were even jagged and serrated like the fine teeth of a surgical hacksaw. These were clearly prestige artefacts of a high quality and made from imported materials. They frequently accompany burials, often in multiples suggesting quiversfull, and are unlikely to have been taken out on the average hunting trip. Four such arrowheads accompanied the cremation at Sarn-y-bryn-caled and what is more they had been used since the points of two had broken off in typical impact fractures. Like the body, these flints had been burnt but they had not completely spalled suggesting that they had been protected from the fiercest and hottest of the flame, perhaps by the flesh in which they had been embedded.

Human sacrifice is always difficult to prove and many more sceptical archaeologists will argue that there is no evidence for it. They are wrong but, to their credit, the evidence is

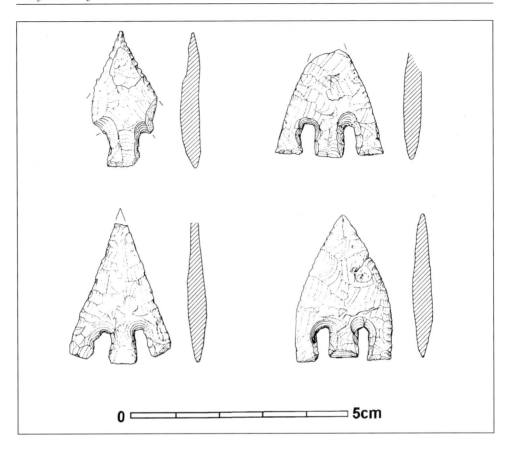

82   The burnt and high-quality flint arrowheads from the primary burial at Sarn-y-bryn-caled, Powys (drawn by Brian Williams © CPAT).

rarely unequivocal. A very close parallel for the burial at Sarn-y-bryn-caled comes from Stonehenge itself where, in the henge ditch, the body of a young man was found lying in a partially crouched position (Evans 1984). Five well-made barbed and tanged arrowheads were found in the ribcage of the skeleton including the point of one which was embedded in the rear of the body's breast bone. From the angle at which the point was embedded, this young man had been shot in the back and this arrow at least had passed through his heart. This arrow certainly would have killed him if the other four had not already done so. Once more from the quality of the arrowheads, from their unnecessarily large numbers and from the final ultimate deposition of this early Bronze Age burial in the ditch of one of the most sacred sites of the period in Britain, this is unlikey to have been a hunting accident. A casualty of war is a possible explanation, but a sacrifice seems more likely **(fig 83)**.

Strabo tells us that the Druids often practised human sacrifice by shooting arrows into the backs of their victims and predicting the future by interpreting the death throes of the victims (Piggott 1975, 110). Strabo's writings, composed at a superstitious time where any

83   Artist's impression of the burial ceremony at Sarn-y-bryn-caled sometime around 2100BC
(by permission of the National Museum of Wales; drawn by Tony Daly, Department of
Archaeology and Numismatics).

practices outside of the Mediterranean were unarguably barbarian, cannot be regarded as
empirical ethnography but, nevertheless, what is important is that he specifies that the
victims were shot in the back. Another important observation is the use of bows and
arrows. The main offensive projectile weapon of the Iron Age Celts was the sling. The
bow appears to have been abandoned. In discussing this, Stuart Piggott (1975), in his book
on *the Druids*, also noted that in the Celtic language of Ireland the words for bows and
arrows are imported from the Norse and Latin suggesting that they are not native artefacts.
Thus this Druidic ritual was undertaken using antiquated weaponry perhaps signifying
the deep-rooted origins of the practice. These deep-respected roots possibly extending
back through the centuries to the third millennium BC.

At Stonehenge, Hawley found a burial pit orientated on the major NE-SW axis of the
phase III monument. Details are sparse and little can be read into this deposit save to
record its presence. This is not the case at nearby Woodhenge where, also aligned on the
main axis and at right angles to it, a low flint cairn covered a pit which contained the
remains of a small child. The line of the midsummer sunrise passed through the centre of
the burial but not through the centre of the pit. Cunnington paints a graphic picture of
the discovery of the child burial:

> When it was first uncovered it was exclaimed 'there must be two skeletons' because there
> appeared to be two skulls lying side by side, touching one another. But when the bones were
> removed they proved to be those of only one individual, and what had looked like two

skulls was actually the two halves of the same skull. It is a common thing to find a skull crushed in the ground, but there seems no way of accounting for its being found lying in two parts, unless it had been cleft before burial (1929, 13).

Cunnington goes on to say that the other bones were articulated and that there appeared to have been no post-depositional disturbance. References to crushed skulls abound in the antiquarian literature and these can normally be explained by the weight of the soil on the fragile bones. But Cunnington is at pains to point out that the skull had been split and not simply crushed and as her husband Benjamin Cunnington, co-director of the excavations, was a medic as well as having considerable excavation experience, we can justifiably accept the observations quoted above.

The head of this small child had been split in two with a stone axe. The two halves had been laid side by side in the central grave of this prestigious monument. Once more the manner of death and the prestige status of the final repository suggest the macabre.

It is therefore possible from the scant remains of potentially unpromising, largely destroyed and eroded sites to recover some of the detail of the doubtless complex rituals that took place at these wooden sanctuaries. We know that feasts were held there or in the immediate surroundings as part of the greater festival, other animal parts may have been used totemically. Deposits were placed at significant points within and around the circle. They involved calendrical and cardinal orientation with a particular observance of the sun. They contained secrets denied to the majority of the population who were excluded from their innermost recesses and indeed care was taken not just to exclude the uninitiated from physically entering the site, but also to prevent visual access through elaborate screens and orientations. They were attended by processions, perhaps in elaborate and colourful costume (though we can only speculate on this) with perhaps masked or bedecked priests, dancers and attendants celebrating the rising sun at its highest and lowest periods, celebrating its warmest and coolest rays, and propitiating its life-giving properties. What the Lord giveth was also taken away at the darker side of some sites. Gruesome ritual executions took place, doubtless infrequently and perhaps only when the population was faced with some major crisis — crop failure, war, drought. Whatever the reason both children and adults appear to have been equally eligible to become part of a ritual which can only be described as the ultimate in structured deposition.

1   The earlier Neolithic house at Ballygally, Antrim, during excavation (courtesy of Derek
     Simpson).

2   A late Neolithic pit at Upper Ninepence, Walton, Radnorshire, during excavation. The pit is
     very shallow but full of pottery, charcoal and flint fragments (© CPAT).

3   The stone circle at Scorhill, Dartmoor.

4   The timber circle at Sarn-y-bryn-caled, Powys, during excavation. The regularity of the circle can be appreciated from this elevated view (© CPAT).

5   *The inner ring of structure 2 at West Kennet, Wiltshire (courtesy of Alisdair Whittle).*

6   *The stone circle of Machrie Moor XI, Arran during excavation. The postholes of the timber circle can be seen as dark patches between the stones (courtesy of Aubrey Burl).*

7   *The recumbent stone circle of Old Keig, Aberdeenshire. Note how the stones decrease in height as they extend away from the recumbent.*

8   *The Shoveldown stone row and terminal multiple circle near Kestor, Dartmoor.*

9   The reconstruction of the Bargeroosterveld temple, Drenthe.

10   The spacing of the uprights in this section of the multiple circle of Woodhenge, Wiltshire, creates a narrow 'window' which marks the direction of the midsummer sunrise.

11   The light box above the entrance of Newgrange which allowed the rays of the rising midwinter sun to penetrate the recesses of the chamber.

12   The timber circle at Knowth during excavation. The postholes were packed with Grooved Ware (courtesy of Derek Simpson).

13 *The large entrance stones at Avebury, Wiltshire. Note how they obscure the entrance.*

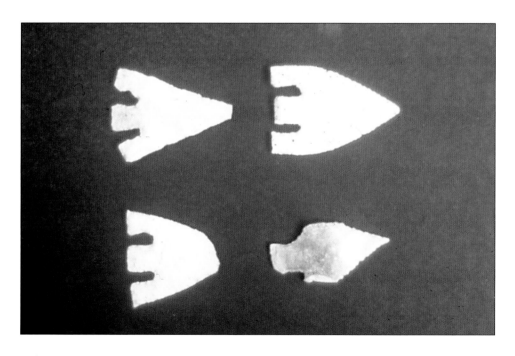

14 *The burnt flint arrowheads from Sarn-y-bryn-caled, Powys. These high-quality missile points were found amongst the cremated bones of the primary burial.*

15   Reconstruction of the Sarn-y-bryn-caled circle within the grounds of the Museum of Welsh
      Life at Cardiff. The reconstruction here is of a series of trilithons rather than a complete circle.

16   The author's preferred reconstruction of Sarn-y-bryn-caled erected for a public open day in
      1991. The entrance posts and the posts of the inner circle were thicker in the original (©
      CPAT).

6 The reconstruction of timber circles

From Stonehenge to Woodhenge and back again

A respected colleague, much more used to dealing with stone circles than wooden ones, uttered the cautionary statement that we cannot deal with timber circles, for the timber does not exist, but rather with circles of postholes. The caution is well-founded, if pessimistic. The distinction between timber circle and posthole circle is a subtle one but nevertheless is one which serves to show our uncertainty as to the appearance and form of the original monument. Stone circle scholars may visit sites and, in the main, be presented with a 4000-year-old monument whose appearance today would be immediately recognisable to its builders and users **(fig 84)**. The site's setting may have changed, now, perhaps, part of a semi-industrialised farming landscape, perhaps on moorland. Internal features may no longer be visible. But neither the heights of the stones nor their overall shape or position need necessarily have changed dramatically.

Even at Stonehenge where time and man have left their obvious marks on the monument, little imagination is necessary to reconstruct the final phase of the circles. Yet Stonehenge has always excited the imagination not least because of its uniqueness **(fig 85)**. No other stone circles match the symmetry and architectural complexity of Stonehenge. None can parallel the degree of dressing of the stones, and none the mighty lintels, each carved to describe a circle rather than a multifaced polygon, and each fixed to its support and to its neighbour by complex jointing. Stonehenge was, and is, a source of inspiration for artists, archaeologists, palaeoastronomers, mathematicians, advocates of natural religion and revellers. It was also a focus, set within a landscape dominated by the armed forces, for the early aerial photographers almost all of whom had a military background **(fig 86)**.

In contrast, the grandeur of timber circles has long since been lost **(fig 87)**. As wood rots and decays, wooden structures need replacement or refurbishment, and through time, timber circles will vanish without surface trace leaving only a legacy of excavated features such as postholes and pits. These deny the satisfying field visits and romantic photography that can emanate from visits to stone circles and indeed timber sites can usually only be viewed from the air; a comparatively recent method of archaeological detection. Even then, they may only appear in favourable conditions. Indeed, it may even be claimed that neither air photography nor geophysical survey can identify timber circles;

84   The Ring of Brodgar.

85   Stonehenge.

86   One of the first aerial photographs of Stonehenge taken by Lieut. Sharpe from a balloon in 1906.

87   John White's late sixteenth-century drawing of Virginian Indians dancing around a timber circle adorned with carved human effigies. As with British Neolithic sites, access to the circle was controlled and in this case it was three chaste beauties who occupied the centre.

they can only identify circles of pits. Only excavation of the monument, even partial or exploratory, can confirm the former presence of posts.

As mentioned above, Stonehenge attracted the early aerial archaeologists from the nearby military installations. It is therefore fitting that during a flight to photograph Stonehenge, the first major archaeological site to be discovered from the air was a circular ditch enclosing concentric ovals of pits; the site was later to become known as Woodhenge **(fig 1)**. Prior to 1925, the site was known as the Dough Cover and with its external bank and internal ditch was considered to be a large but otherwise unremarkable disc barrow. On 12 December 1925, Squadron Leader Insall noted 'white chalk marks in the centre' of the circle. A pioneer of aerial photography with an uncannily early knowledge of cropmark formation processes, Insall kept the site under observation 'to see what the crops would reveal'. His prescience was rewarded, for in July 'five or six or perhaps seven closely-set rings of spots appeared' in the ripening wheat. Cunnington (1929) records a subsequent site visit which noted the different patches of dense wheat, particularly over the ditch, and records that this was a phenomenon commonly noted by the agricultural labourers, particularly at harvest time, but that the import of the phenomenon had generally escaped enquiry.

Excavation followed between 1926 and 1928 and the dark wheat patches proved to cover six ovals of pits. Each pit was shown to have held a post. The largest posts were in the third oval from the outside, Ring C, and these were also the largest pits seen on Insall's stunningly clear photograph.

The Dough Cover became 'Woodhenge' during the course of the excavation 'when the nature of the site was gradually revealing itself'. No one person was accredited with the renaming and indeed Cunnington records that the name was not devised but rather developed as the excavations progressed. Cunnington went on to draw serious comparison with Stonehenge. The maximum diameters of the Woodhenge ovals compared favourably with the Stonehenge settings and of course there were the orientations on cardinal points and the midsummer sunrise. Cunnington also noted that 'it has been suggested that the uprights of the C ring supported wooden cross beams or lintels, analogous to those at Stonehenge. This seems not improbable, but there is of course no direct evidence for or against it.'

Cunnington argued that Stonehenge was the later monument and that Woodhenge was the earlier prototype. In this hypothesis she quoted mainly the more refined nature of Stonehenge but also quoted the observation of other, earlier commentators. Petrie, in 1882, had noted that 'Stonehenge by its tenons and mortices is an evident imitation of wooden architecture', and E.H. Stone had also voiced the opinion that this architectural device suggested a wooden prototype. Both sources were quoted by Cunnington in her excavation report (1929). Cunnington summed up the current theses:

> *It has been conjectured on purely technical grounds that Stonehenge must have had a wooden prototype. It has also often been said that Stonehenge seems to stand alone and to have nothing intermediate between it and the comparatively crude and simple stone circles. Is it not possible that this apparent lack of ancestry is due to the fact that the more immediate forerunners of Stonehenge were of timber and have perished? (1929, 20)*

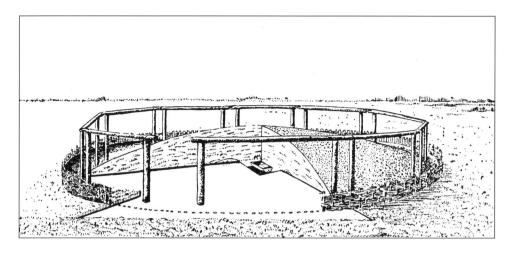

88   van Giffen's reconstruction of the timber circle around the Hooge Mierde barrow.

This is a compelling argument and one to which we shall return.

Meanwhile, across the North Sea, post circles were being found in increasing numbers below the early bronze age barrows of the northern Netherlands (van Giffen 1930; 1938). Their function was puzzling but the post voids found in the gleyed turf mounds of the barrows showed that they had clearly protruded through the mound and must have been visible as post circles round the margin of the barrow. The Dutch monuments varied considerably from single post rings to double stake circles and multiple arrangements of closely set posts. Van Giffen looked to both Britain and Germany for parallels for the Dutch sites. Britain provided the closest analogies for the Dutch circles, not only from within barrows but also within monuments that would later become known as henges. Following Cunnington to the degree of calling these British sites 'Woodhenges', van Giffen reconstructed the outer wooden circles at Wessinghuizen and Hooge Mierde near Groningen as lintelled structures using mortice and tenon jointing to fix the lintels to the regularly spaced uprights **(fig 88)**.

By 1930, Cunnington and her husband were excavating a second multiple timber circle at the Sanctuary on Overton Hill. Seven broadly concentric timber rings were located, apparently set around a flimsy yet deep-set (42in. or *c.*1.5m) central post **(fig 89)**. Cunnington considered the possibility that the circle complex represented a roofed building, perhaps with a thatched roof. 'The idea suggested itself mainly on account of the strength implied by the size and depth of the post holes, the twin posts in the Bank Holiday ring (4th from the inside, Ring D) and the fact of a central post' (p309, my brackets). Cunnington clearly stated that there were difficulties in utilising all elements of the site in the roofed reconstructions but that plans had been drawn up in which the double ring had been utilised either as a device to support the ends of rafters or as supports for log walling. While perhaps an attractive idea, Cunnington was not, however, convinced that the Sanctuary was ever roofed. Had such been the intention 'the ground plan would have been simpler as any roof using all these uprights is necessarily a complicated

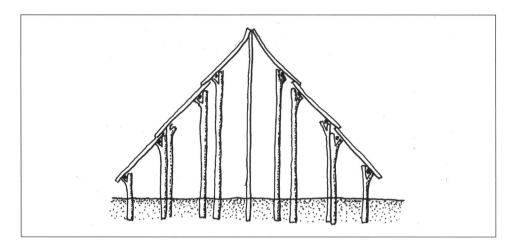

89   Cunnington's hypothesis for the roofing of the Sanctuary.

structure. On the whole, therefore, it is felt that the arguments against there having been a roof is stronger than those in favour of one' (309). The argument was clearly an on-going one, however, and the following year Lt-Col. R.H. Cunnington, nephew of Maud and Benjamin, proposed that the spacing of the post rings might well suit a series of three overlapping roof sections, an hypothesis which suited the double postholes of the 'Bank Holiday' ring **(fig 89)**.

In 1935, Grahame Clark excavated a henge monument at Arminghall in Norfolk (Clark 1936). This site had also been discovered accidentally by Wing Commander Insall, three years after his discovery of Woodhenge. Dark patches arranged in a horseshoe within the monument proved to be substantial postholes 2-2.25m (6ft 8in-7ft 6in) deep from which it was inferred that the posts stood to a considerable height — perhaps as much as 6m above the ground and weighing close on 4 tonnes. Clark discussed the likelihood that the posts carried lintels in a trilithon arrangement, again quoting the mortise and tenon joints at Stonehenge and, of course, at about this time a presumed Neolithic or Bronze Age morticed beam had been found on the submerged Lyonesse land surface in Essex proving that the prehistorians' assumed wood technology did indeed exist (Warren *et al.* 1936). Returning to Arminghall, however, Clark concluded that there was no evidence in the arrangement of the postholes to suggest pairing. In proposing a ritual function for the henge monuments, Clark concluded that the timbers at Arminghall 'were not the uprights of a house, but the pillars, as it were, of an open-air temple'.

Writing in 1937, a French scholar, Vayson de Pradenne, suggested analogy with the native north American earth lodges to illustrate the former appearance not just of timber circles but Stonehenge as well (Vayson de Pradenne 1937). Stonehenge's outer sarsen circle and innner, higher, sarsen horseshoe resembled, in his mind, the architectural skeleton of an Omaha earth lodge and the roofing technology and logistics would not be beyond the capabilities of peoples who had raised 40-ton sarsens and placed on them 7-ton lintels. Vayson de Pradenne's arguments have not, however, found general acceptance

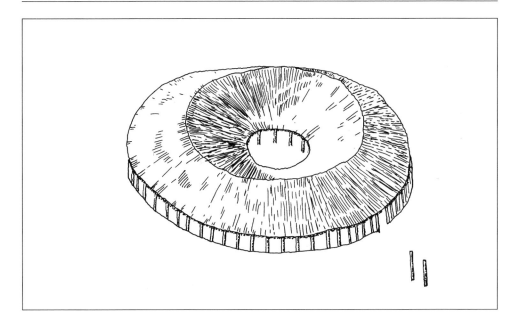

90   *Piggott's isometric reconstruction of Woodhenge with central oculus. This reconstruction had a profound influence on timber circle interpretation.*

though the earth lodge analogy has since been transcribed to other timber circles.

In 1940, Stuart Piggott returned to the roofed hypothesis and started with the assumption that the multiple rings at the Sanctuary did not represent a single phased monument. At the Sanctuary, Piggott considered that the smallest circle, circle F and the central post probably represented a small hut about 4.5m (15ft) in diameter and with a central roof support; Cunnington's original suggestion. Phase II was represented by the postrings D and E, the double nature of which was taken to represent replacement by analogy with the iron age house at Little Woodbury. The resulting building had an open roof or *impluvium* necessitating the replacement of posts in both rings. The original hut may have been 'enshrined' by phase II. Phase II comprised rings B,C and G complete with the stones spaced between the uprights of ring C. This formed a large circular building with the large posts of ring G representing a raised 'lantern' or clerestory.

Piggott drew analogy with Brazilian round houses as well as drawing on Vayson de Pradenne's Omaha Indian earth lodges. The practice of enshrining former buildings had Christian parallels and the central opening was reminiscent of the *oculus* in the Pantheon in Rome.

Piggott's roofing hypothesis could be extended to Woodhenge. The large posts of ring C with their attendant ramps suggested a primacy of erection since the ramps made it unlikely that they could have been set upright while the other posts were standing. Piggott's reconstruction utilised these massive posts as supporting a ridge pole with the roof sloping down on either side to an outer wall and inner *impluvium*. The Globe theatre at Southwark was invoked as a parallel **(fig 90)**.

Piggott was at pains to point out that he did not regard his roofed building theory as relevant to all timber circles. Bleasdale and Arminghall were clearly not roofed in his opinion and again ethnographic parallels were invoked, for example John White's drawing (c.1585) of Virginian Indians dancing around a circle of timber uprights carved with human representations **(fig 87)**. Piggott makes the pertinent statement 'that in archaeology there are always several correct explanations for any set of observed phenomena' (1940, 217).

In so saying, Piggott more or less admits that the reconstruction of timber circles is largely a matter of personal preference. But there are, at all sites, certain absolute facts that may be used: namely the depths of the postholes, the spacing of the postholes and the widths of the posts as revealed by the post-pipes. From these frugal data, skeletons may be constructed — the thickness of the posts, their heights (using the generally accepted 1:3 below ground to above ground ratio) and their arrangement. Like the dinosaurs before them these basic timber skeletons may then be fleshed out using almost palaeontological hypothesis.

The most objective and comprehensive study of the roofing hypothesis was undertaken by an architect turned archaeologist, Chris Musson, who used his formal training to undertake a feasibility study following the excavation of the complex timber circles at Durrington Walls (Musson in Wainwright & Longworth 1971).

Musson had to deal with the ground plans and the skeletal data outlined above **(fig 91)**. He pointed out that much of a building's design was likely to have been influenced by its intended function and by the traditions which gave rise to it: these are archaeologically invisible. Furthermore the possible phasing of these timber circles is also a matter of question, there rarely being any stratigraphical data surviving to suggest discrete sequences: the priority of one ring over another may represent little more than a building sequence, a phasing measured in hours rather than years. Already there was a difficulty of interpretation, were these multiple circles single or multi-phased? If the latter, what was their phasing?

The Northern Circle at Durrington Walls (where two distinct phases could be determined stratigraphically) was capable in phase 2 of reconstruction as a roughly circular building (with slightly flattened sides) around a central square which could have supported some central lantern-type structure. The reconstruction is feasible but 'the search for clues to confirm or deny this interpretation is, however, inconclusive'. Indeed, it was argued later that the ground plan of the Northern Circle resembled that of phase 1 of the Southern Circle though at this latter site the central posts were too slender to allow a lantern roof interpretation. Thus 'if the apparent similarity is other than coincidental, a significant doubt must be thrown on the roofed interpretation for the Northern Circle'.

The first phase of the Southern Circle could also be interpreted as a single roofed structure however some of the posts appeared too flimsy, some being only 15cm in diameter, and they were inadequately spaced. Some of the spans envisaged also seem excessive for the slenderness of the posts generally. In conclusion 'a fully roofed interpretation ... seems doubtful though ... (not) ... absolutely impossible' (my brackets). A partially roofed structure, perhaps sloping inwards, was suggested as an alternative. The second phase of this Southern Circle is more complete forming a complex 6-ring

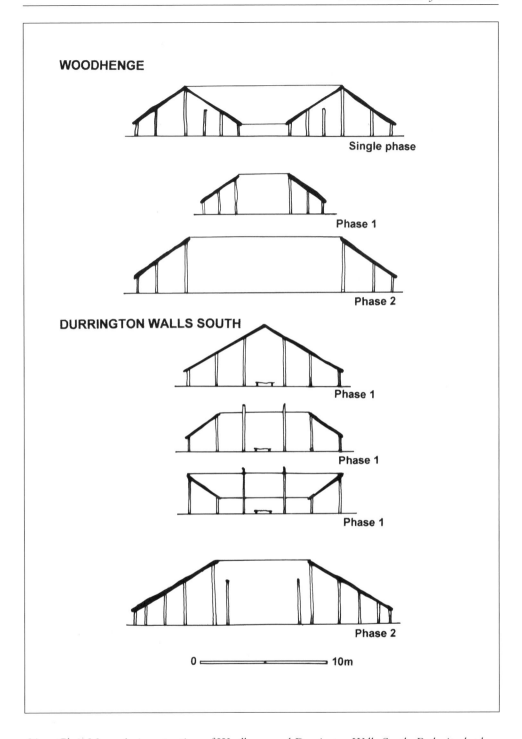

91   *Chris Musson's reconstructions of Woodhenge and Durrington Walls South. Both sites lend themselves to several different schemes, all of which, according to Musson, were possible, but probably unlikely.*

structure of near concentric rings of posts. The general progress in height and proportions of the posts towards the interior suggested an outward sloping roof though the flimsiness of the innermost posts suggested that they were non-structural and that the roof had, therefore, a central *oculus* or opening.

Despite Musson's clear introductory statement to the effect that 'the aim of this appendix is not to produce definitive reconstructions of the timber circles at Durrington Walls, but rather to investigate the variety of possible building forms ...', his hypothetical reconstructions have become enshrined in stone, are generally accepted without question and have been reproduced, redrawn and remodified (often carelessly and unintentionally) in much of the relevant archaeological literature of the last quarter century. The negative arguments which Musson produced in his appendix have largely been ignored: elements which did not fit readily into any roofed reconstruction, non-radial arrangements of posts (radially arranged uprights would have considerably facilitated roofing), the unnecessary depth of some postholes, and flimsier than expected uprights in some areas. Indeed, Musson's conclusion that '... the best hope of an all-embracing explanation may lie in the idea of ritual or symbolic settings of free-standing posts ...' has found less favour than his attractive reconstructions, and was even ignored in the conclusion of the Durrington Walls report in which Musson's study forms an appendix. Interestingly, Musson also drew analogy with Stonehenge.

Almost a decade later, Roger Mercer made an important contribution to the study of the reconstruction of timber circles in the discussion section of his excavation of the much eroded henge and timber circle at Balfarg, Fife. In this article, Mercer looked objectively at the dimensions of the postholes of various circles in an attempt to estimate the heights to which the posts stood. He used as a starting point the lengths of the post ramps at Durrington Walls and Woodhenge circle F. Mercer assumed that the ramps would be used to overtopple the posts so that the outer edge of the ramp would be at the centre of balance of the post. Thus the distance from the inner edge of the posthole to the outer edge of the ramp would be about half the total length of the post. Comparison of this assumed post length with the depth of the postholes gave a general ratio of 1:3 or 1:3.5; that is that if the posthole was 1m deep the total post length was 3-3.5m and that therefore 2-2.5m stood above ground. When this model was strictly applied, it suggested that any roof pitch would need to be shallower than suggested by Musson's reconstructions and it also suggested a great variation in post height even within individual post rings. This in itself is not conclusive evidence against the roofed hypothesis since Musson pointed out that posts need not be so deeply sunk if they are to be load-bearing elements of a unified structure than they would have been were they intended to be free-standing posts. Nevertheless, Mercer also recalled Cunnington's observation that the stone sockets at Stonehenge had been dug to varying depths to ensure that differently sized stones presented a level top sufficiently horizontal to receive the lintels. Mercer wondered 'whether we should place this consideration alongside the many other carpentry parallels at this unique site to reassess the nature of some of the timber circles located within British henge monuments'.

The excavation of the timber circle at Sarn-y-bryn-caled in mid-Wales gave just such an opportunity. It was noted at this site that the posts had been carefully placed at the centre

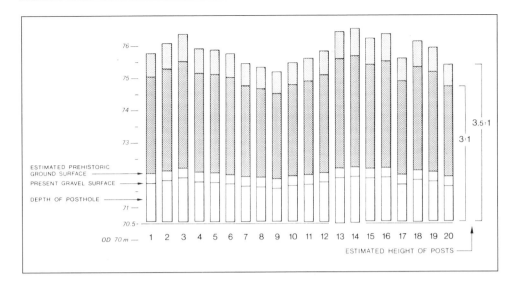

92   *The proposed heights of the Sarn-y-bryn-caled uprights based on a 1:3 and 1:3.5 ratio for the posthole depth/post height (drawing by Brian Williams © CPAT).*

of each of the postholes, not up against one side as might be expected. It was also noted that the posthole depths varied and so, therefore, might we expect the heights of the posts to vary also **(fig 92)**. However, the timber circle stood on a gravel terrace above the present floodplain of the River Severn and the top of this gravel terrace was seen to be rounded. The bases of the postholes moreover were all demonstrated to be roughly at the same height above sea level. It is possible, therefore, that the differing depths of the postholes might be accounted for by their situation relative to the rise and fall of the gravel surface **(fig 93)**. In other words, if the postholes were designed to receive posts cut to equal length, and if the intention of the builders was to create a level upper platform on which, for example, to place some form of entablature, then the Sarn-y-bryn-caled postholes were excellently surveyed and ensured just such an end result.

During the reconstruction of the timber circle at Sarn-y-bryn-caled, a 1:3/3.5 ratio was also reached by the less mathematical method of asking local farmers and fencers the simple question 'how deep would you bed in a free-standing post?'. The answer clearly varied according to the individual's experience but there was broad agreement that a 6ft high post would need to be sunk at least 2ft into the ground. The 1:3 ratio therefore was not posthole depth to total post length but posthole depth to post height above ground. This, in effect, increases Mercer's formula to 1:4 and so his 1:3.5 may be accepted as a compromise. Indeed logic dictates that Mercer's calculations are cautious since in prehistory one is unlikely to be dealing with modern trimmed posts but with trees which would have widened towards the base. This would have given greater stability to the post if erected with the thicker base portion downwards and also would seriously have affected the post length to post ramp ratio since the centre of gravity of a felled tree bole is usually towards the bottom third rather than halfway along its length (inf from Peter Reynolds).

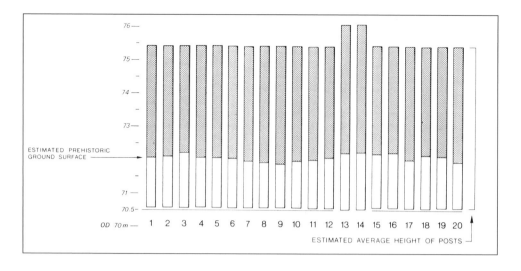

93   *Proposed heights of the Sarn-y-bryn-caled uprights using an average post size and after considering the absolute depths of the postholes and the natural rise and fall of the gravel terrace (drawing by Brian Williams © CPAT).*

Through the generous cooperation of Powis Estates, it was possible to procure sufficient oak boles to effect a full-scale reconstruction based on the above observations. In the course of one of the wettest days of a mid-Wales February, 26 oak posts were erected in the centres of postholes which had last seen such use almost 4000 years earlier. This time modern hydraulics were used to erect the posts and chainsaws ensured their equal length. The excavations of the circle completed, it had been confirmed during the various planning phases that the circle was regular in its plan with evenly-spaced posts and a truly circular design. This circularity was clearly the intention of the prehistoric architects yet when the uprights were in position, the circularity of the monument was not at all obvious **(fig 94)**. Instead, the reconstruction appeared, from ground level, to be a jumble of posts emanating from a base whose ground plan was not at all obvious. Lintels were added and at once the circularity of the monument was obvious **(fig 95)**.

It cannot be proven. Direct evidence does not survive. It cannot be disproven for exactly the same reasons. Yet from Cunnington, the first student of timber circles, through van Giffen, Musson and Mercer, lintels seem to be the preferred reconstruction. Indeed at Balfarg and North Mains the excavators argued that the differing depths of the postholes was a device to ensure a horizontal entablature when using posts of unequal length: the theory is an attractive one and, it would appear, can be supported by any data. Indeed the attractiveness of the theory and the obvious Stonehenge parallels have gained acceptance as evidenced by the increasing number of lintelled reconstructions proposed in recent years.

More recent timber circle excavations have continued the debate. In Ireland, the excavator of the Ballynahatty circle beside the Giant's Ring henge in County Down preferred a lintelled reconstruction (Hartwell 1998) while at Knowth in County Meath, a roofed interpretation is favoured **(fig 96)**. Bourke's argument for a ridge-roofed structure

94   The Sarn-y-bryn-caled circle during reconstruction. Note how freestanding posts do not convey the circularity of the monument (photo © CPAT).

95   The reconstructed circle at Sarn-y-bryn-caled complete with lintels. The circularity of the structure is now much more apparent (photo © CPAT).

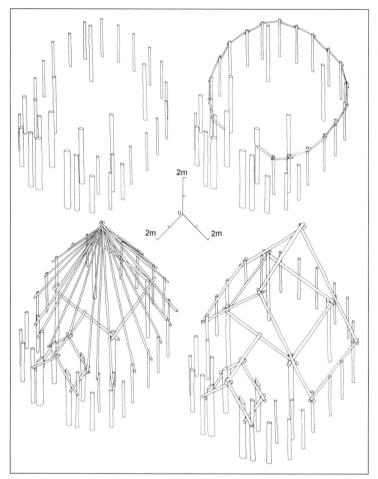

96 Bourke's various reconstructions of the Knowth timber circle (courtesy of George Eogan).

at Knowth is based on the arrangement of the postholes, their depths and the deposition of artefacts within them (in Eogan & Roche 1997). The Knowth circle is also comparable in size with domestic structures of the period and therefore roofing of this edifice was entirely within the technological capabilities of the contemporary population. Bourke's reconstruction also necessitates no complex joinery even though we know from waterlogged sites such as the Lyonesse land surface in Essex where a morticed plank was found, from Storrs Moss, Lancashire where a tenon was found and from the enigmatic monument at Bargeroosterveld in the Netherlands **(colour plate 9)** that such joinery did exist at the time of timber circles. At Knowth, four internal postholes set in a rectangular arrangement were interpreted as roof supports **(fig 97)**. At Ballynahatty, an ostensibly morphologically very similar circle, the inner postholes were interpreted as the uprights of a mortuary platform. Whereas the differing posthole data can be quoted as evidence for the same result — that is to ensure the post tops were level, so here at Ballynahatty and Knowth, the same data can be interpreted very differently. There is little doubt that personal preference appears to be the predominant force in the reconstruction of these fascinating monuments **(colour plate 15)**.

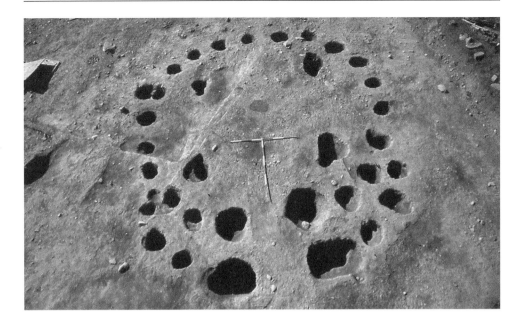

97   The Knowth timber circle during excavation (photo Helen Roche; courtesy of George Eogan).

Perhaps the argument is unanswerable, at least until a perfectly preserved, for example waterlogged, site is found in one of the many peatlands in Britain and Ireland. Hopes of such a find were raised by the discovery of a waterlogged site at Holme-next-the-sea in Norfolk. This site was originally on land but, due to relative sea level rises, was now below high-water mark. The subterranean timbers of the circular palisade had survived in their waterlogged environment and proved to have been split oak. At the centre of the circle, an upturned oak bole had been inserted into the pit so that the lower part of the trunk and the remains of the roots projected a short distance above the original ground level. Broad-edged metal axe marks on the wood, and dendrochronological and radiocarbon dating indicate that the monument was built around 2000BC but unfortunately all above-ground timbers had been lost; there was no artefactual material associated with the site and the direct contextual association had also been scoured away by tidal action. Speculation as to the function of this site has been rife. The central oak has been interpreted as a tree burial, exposure platform or altar. The entrance was provided by a forked branch in the SW arc. However, at only 6m in diameter, the Holme site has far closer parallels with palisaded round barrows in this country and the Netherlands than it does with timber circles. It is not inconceivable, indeed it is likely, that the timbers were intended as revetments for a straight-sided barrow mound, that this material then collapsed as the timbers rotted and has, like the context of the site, been washed away. Unfortunately the potential of Holme for timber circle studies has not materialised.

It is possible that a peculiar Dutch site may be able to offer us more information regarding the above-ground appearance of timber circles. The site at Bargeroosterveld was found in a raised bog near Emmen in the province of Drenthe in the northern

98   Detail of the reconstructed lintels of the temple at Bargeroosterveld, Drenthe.

Netherlands (Waterbolk & van Zeist 1961). Here a peculiar, almost Japanese-looking, monument with pagoda-like protruding lintels was found during peat cutting in 1957. Within a circle of small rounded boulders were set two planks each with a line of four rectangular mortice holes cut in them. These planks measure almost 2m in length, they were split from an oak trunk of approximately 0.8m in diameter and had been laid directly on the bog surface with underlying thin wedges of wood to ensure that they were level. The four corner posts each had a tenon some 0.75m long after which the post was rectangular. The inner posts also had tenons, but of only about half the length of the corner posts, and were circular. Two smaller oak trunks, from oak 30cm in diameter, stood between the planks to complete the sides of a square. The whole monument had probably been floored with sand. Wood cutting debris in the vicinity showed that the timbers had been trimmed on site. Curved and rectangular-sectioned pieces each with a rectangular mortice hole and rectangular rebate were also found and appear to have been from lintels over the uprights: there was no suggestion of a roof **(fig 98)**. Waterbolk drew parallels for this monument from the rectangular post arrangements often found in Urnfield barrows however, with a radiocarbon date of 1420-1050 Cal BC, the site falls at the end of the timber circle tradition in Britain and the Netherlands: has the circle been squared?

Whether the Bargeroosterveld structure marks the end of the decline of the circle tradition, as four-posters do in stone circles, or whether it is the Adam and Eve of Urnfield sepulchral architecture is largely irrelevant since at present it is a unique site. What is more relevant to the timber circle argument is the accomplished joinery which it exhibits. The rebates to allow the lintels to cross, the squaring of the corner uprights, and the horned terminals hint at far more refined prehistoric woodworking than most modern reconstructions — poles lashed with string — allow.

99   *Stonehenge.*

This brings us back full circle to Stonehenge and the observations made by Cunnington and her contemporaries. Stonehenge is not a crude stone circle with rectangular lintels 'plonked' on top of rectangular uprights. It is a sophisticated edifice whose elements are all specifically designed to contribute to the overall plan of the monument **(fig 99)**. Thus, the sarsen uprights have the flatter, better dressed, of their two wider faces on the inner circumference of the circle they describe, the lintels are similarly curved to form a circle rather than a multi-sided polygon. This attention to detail illustrates a number of elements. Firstly it highlights the advanced planning of the monument and the architectural vision of its designers. Secondly it demonstrates that the monument as we see it today was a precise concept. And thirdly it illustrates the technological achievement of the prehistoric population and the effectiveness of primitive tools when used by people who know their capabilities and how to use them.

The complexity of Stonehenge clearly attests that it is part of a well-founded and established tradition. On the site itself the developmental sequence has been recently redefined (Cleal *et al.* 1995). Phase 1 (*c.*3000 BC) comprises the ditch and the Aubrey hole circle, probably containing posts — a ditched timber circle. Phase 2 (*c.* 2900-2550 BC) sees the dismantling of the timber circle in the Aubrey holes, the first appearance of cremations at the site and the construction in the interior of a number of timber settings. The exact layout of these posthole arrangements is difficult to determine as a result of the destruction of many by subsequent remodellings of the site. Cleal *et al.*, however, make an excellent case for circular arrangements and, by linking postholes of similar depths and diameters, have proposed a number of possible timber rings. This may not be a completely reliable method, however, given the variation in depth of postholes within a single ring already noted at Balfarg, Durrington Walls and North Mains. Nevertheless, it appears that at sometime prior to 2500 BC, there was a multiple timber circle on the site now occupied by the sarsen and bluestone circles **(fig 37)**. This complex was approached by an avenue of paired posts, 3m wide and 16m long, leading down to the southern entrance and crossed by a possible screen running east-west across the avenue. This arrangement clearly resembles the similar multiple circles with avenues and screens at the northern and southern circles at Durrington Walls, only some 2 miles (3km) to the north-east and, further afield, at Lugg in Co. Dublin.

This avenue and traces of a possible double circle were discussed by Burl (1987) based on far less evidence than was ultimately available to Cleal. Burl envisaged a double circle (though the outer one was represented by but a single posthole) which he interpreted as a mortuary house. This interpretation is doubtless influenced by Hawley's own observation that the avenue and internal posthole arrangements resembled a 'wooden passage grave'. A thorough scrutiny of the antiquarian diggings at Stonehenge led Burl to note that human remains, as well as those of 'several sorts of beasts as appears by the heads of diverse kinds of them', had been documented by Inigo Jones and recovered through the centuries from the centre of the circle and this in turn lead him to draw analogy with the long barrows and mortuary structures of the earlier Neolithic where ox skulls in particular are well represented. Accordingly, Burl interpreted the structure as a charnel house, where the inedible parts of animals, notably their skulls, accompanied the human dead.

This is really stretching the evidence. Unfortunately, excavations, ancient and modern, at Stonehenge have not kept records which are expected of a modern excavation. Later rebuilding at Stonehenge has in any case destroyed much of what evidence might have survived. But, using much data inaccessible to Burl, Cleal *et al.* have located more postholes in what may probably have been circular settings. Few, if any, had ramps. It appears more likely, though it is doubtful if it will ever be proven, that the site contained a multiple timber circle than it did a double-walled charnel house. A multiple circle would find more local parallels at Woodhenge, and Durrington Walls and, as has been pointed out animal bones have been found in significant quantities at both sites.

In phase 3 at Stonehenge, the timber settings were replaced in stone. The Q and R holes were excavated, the sarsens were erected, possibly associated with a lintelled setting of bluestones, replaced, about 2000 BC, with the present horseshoe and circular bluestone setting. Quite aside from the argument relating to the bluestones' origins, one conclusion is clear and that is that at least some of the bluestones were originally set in a lintelled arrangement. Evidence for this comes from the remains of bluestones 67, 69, 70 and 36 **(fig 100)** which exhibit respectively tenons and mortices. Bluestone 70, now forming part of the inner bluestone horseshoe, has on its top, the remains of the stump of a tenon as do, to a lesser extent, stones 67 and 69. Bluestone 36 is particularly well-dressed and well-formed with two deep, circular mortice holes. This stone is now partly buried but the mortices are still visible, just peeping above the present grassline. What is not known, however, is whether this lintelled structure represented a circle or a series of trilithons. If the latter then a parallel may be drawn with timber circles such as Lugg and Goldington where pairs of postholes may well be the remains of trilithons or, more accurately, trixylons. If the former, then it may suggest that the multiple timber circles in Britain were, like Stonehenge 3iii, comprised of various lintelled circles of varying heights. It also

100   The mortice holes in the partly buried Bluestone 36 attesting that at least some of the bluestones had originally been arranged in a lintelled setting.

suggests the presence of lintelled timber structures in Britain from as early as *c*.2500 BC, and more likely far earlier.

The sarsen and bluestone horseshoe settings may also be paralleled in timber circles. Firstly sites such as Woodhenge, Cairnpapple and Dorchester 3 are oval and not circular. But more closely Machrie Moor I has an internal horseshoe open to the south-west. The Machrie Moor horseshoe comprises five posts, larger in diameter than those of the outer circles. Arminghall is also a horseshoe setting comprising eight large posts with their opening to the south-west. The even number of posts at this site tempt the interpretation as lintelled pairs.

It is now that we return to the mortice and tenon and tongue and groove joints on the Stonehenge lintels and sarsens **(fig 101)**. The lintels at Stonehenge are fixed to their uprights with mortice and tenon joints. Moreover, they are fixed to each other with tongue and groove joints. That these are wood-working techniques is an observation that has been made numerous times before. The question that has rarely been asked is 'why?'. Why was it necessary to continuously pound, day after wearing day, at the top of a sarsen to crush away the majority of the stone while leaving one (or two in the case of the outer circle) large rounded tenon standing proud of the top of the stone? Why was it necessary to exercise much effort and spend considerable time hollowing out two mortice holes on the under side of each lintel **(fig 102)**? (Indeed, time and effort was expounded on hollowing mortice holes on **both** sides of the inner trilithon lintel 156, a cautionary example of quality control in the late Neolithic.) Why was it necessary to ensure that each

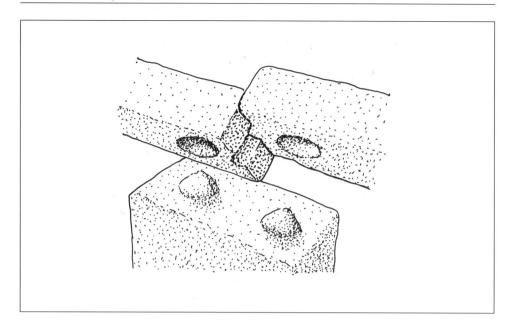

101   *Schematic diagram indicating the methods used to fit the lintels of the Sarsen ring (after Richards).*

102   *The mortice holes in the fallen lintel, Stone 156. This stone has mortice holes in the upper surface too suggesting that mistakes could also happen in Prehistory.*

103   The interior of Stonehenge. Tenons can be clearly seen on the tops of the uprights.

lintel could be fixed to its neighbour by laboriously fashioning a tongue at one end and a groove at the other? The fact is, that the prehistoric builders of Stonehenge were completely wasting their collective time! Weighing in at approximately 7 tonnes, the lintels at Stonehenge needed no fixing. Their sheer weight, if placed on flat surfaces, would have ensured that they stayed in place. It is much more likely that these architectural devices were used because that was the tradition within which Stonehenge's builders were working. The Stonehenge lintels were fixed to their uprights in a manner usual in such monuments. This is how it *was* done, not how it needed to be done **(fig 103)**.

There is another explanation. The mortice and tenon joints, unlike the norm in joinery, do not completely pierce the stone. They are not mortice and tenon *sensu stricto* but ball and socket joints allowing the stones to swivel. Thus, when lowering the lintels into position, the ball and sockets would have engaged and acted as a self-righting mechanism, guiding the lintels into their precise positions with far less effort than would have been necessary were they to have been levered to and fro in an attempt to exact their positioning.

Stonehenge is a unique site with no obvious parallels either in Britain or abroad. Yet the preconceived design presumes earlier prototypes. The joinery techniques used, also suggest that these prototypes were in timber. Timber circles are also frequently replaced in stone. This certainly appears to have happened at Stonehenge though in this case the design of the final monument appears to be much closer to the original wooden sites than do the majority of other 'lithicisations'. It is argued here, therefore, that Stonehenge is not a stone circle — a class of monument in which no direct parallels can be found — but in fact a timber circle, though made unusually of stone. If this is the case, then timber circles do survive and their reconstruction need involve no theoretical hypotheses.

The similarity does not end there, however. In 1926, Hawley discovered a burial at the centre of Stonehenge. This had been badly disturbed by earlier riflings but the pit lay

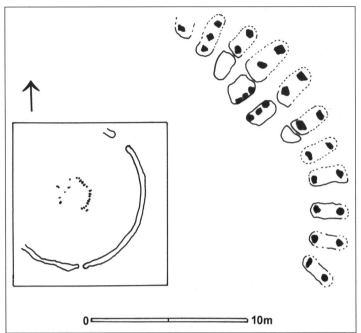

*104   General plan
and detail of the
Q&R hole settings
at Stonehenge (after
Cleal et al.)
reminiscent of the
double postholes at
the Sanctuary.*

0 ▭▭▭▭▭▭ **10m**

along the major NE-SW axis of the monument and was marked by a post. This recalls the child sacrifice at Woodhenge, marked by a cairn, in the centre of the monument and aligned on the main axis. The Stonehenge burial cannot be dated, but the multiple postholes, the central axially aligned burial and the abundant animal remains do suggest a closer parallel with Woodhenge than has hitherto been admitted.

There are also curious arrangements in the first phases of the stone monument at Stonehenge which are reminiscent of timber circles. The Q and R holes, excavated some time around 2500 BC, comprised an oval of 'dumbell-shaped' pits, each effectively two conjoined stoneholes designed to hold a pair of bluestones set radially. It is unlikely that this phase was ever finished since the setting forms only an arc around the eastern side of the circle. Indeed, it is not even true to say that they form an arc, but rather an arc in the south-east quadrant and almost a straight line in the north-east. If ever the intention was to construct a circle of such pairs, it would have had a remarkably flattened circumference **(fig 104)**. The pairing is unusual, however, and draws immediate parallel with ring D at Woodhenge which comprises oval, effectively double, postholes each of which contained two posts set radially. Two roughly contemporary monuments, less than 2 miles (3km) apart, sharing such a similar yet unusual architectural feature is hardly likely to be entirely coincidental.

There is also a pair of bluestones at Stonehenge which are remarkable for their unusual shapes. Stones 66 and 68, located in the south-west arc of the inner bluestone horseshoe are set either side of the NE-SW axis and opposite the north-east entrance. Stone 66 is represented only by a stump and has a well-defined ridge running down what remains of its length. This ridge, or tongue, has been deliberately formed by the chipping away and pounding of the stone on either side to leave the ridge standing proud. Stone 68, in contrast, has a groove running down its length into which the ridge of stone 66 would

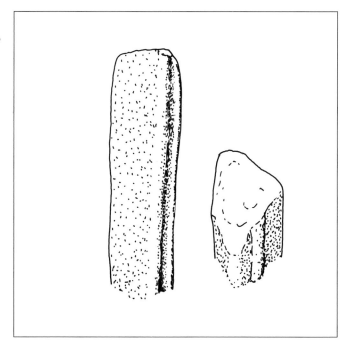

105   Bluestones 68 and 66, presumably designed to fit together (after Cleal et al.).

have fitted **(fig 105)**. In their present positions, the stones are some 3m apart and the tongue of 66 faces south-east while the groove of 68 faces north-west. Currently appearing to shun each other, Atkinson (1979) suggested that in an earlier arrangement these stones may well have formed a joined pair standing in almost conjungal togetherness within the same as yet unlocated stonehole.

This is yet another feature found within the timber circle tradition. At Dorchester 3 **(fig 106)** two posts shared a posthole in the south-south-west of the monument. At Poole in Dorset, postholes 3 and 11 in the south and north respectively contained two posts and at Dorchester V and VI double posts were found in the north-west and south-east arcs respectively. Confined to the Thames Valley and Wessex, this pairing may represent a regional architectural tradition surviving as posthole evidence at timber circles and lithicised at Stonehenge.

These features, the joinery techniques used to fix the lintels in both the sarsen and earlier bluestone phases, the trilithions, the central axially aligned burial, the paired stone- and postholes, combined with Cunnington's original observations as to the dimensional similarities between Stonehenge and Woodhenge suggest to the present writer at least that Stonehenge may be more representative of the original appearance of timber circles than can be inferred from the wooden evidence alone.

What else about the original appearance of timber circles may we glean from the scant archaeological evidence? The answer is not a great deal. It is possible that the gaps between the postholes were not open but filled with fencing of some description. For example, some circles have their entrances elaborated in some ways: the porch/screen arrangements at Ballynahatty and Knowth, for example, the larger entrance posts at Durrington Walls and Sarn-y-bryn-caled, the wider entrance passage at Woodhenge and the avenues

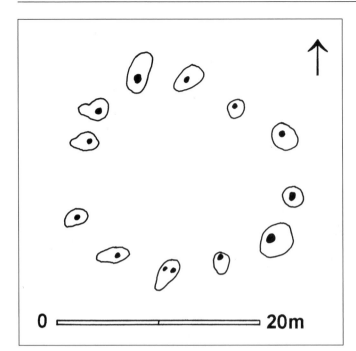

106   Plan of the timber circle at Dorchester 3, Oxfordshire with evidence for two posts sharing the same posthole (after Bradley & Chambers).

approaching Durrington Walls, Lugg, Stonehenge, Poole and Ogden Down. That these entrances were elaborated may suggest that they were the only intended means of entry, if not the only possible means of entry. Were the other gaps between the postholes plugged? It is a possibility but proof is lacking. Hurdle screening, for example, would leave scant if any archaeological traces, wattle and daub might be expected to leave some remains of clay yet many circles, for example on gravel terraces, have already lost significant amounts of their original stratigraphy as a result of agricultural degradation. With timber circles, we are dealing with bare skeletal detail.

But interestingly, fragments of planking were found at North Mains, Ballynahatty and Dorchester. These fragmentary remains were just that, very fragmentary, and they can hardly be regarded as conclusive data but their presence may be significant and may well suggest solid barriers between the posts restricting access and vision to the interior by any way other than the prescribed route. At Sarn-y-bryn-caled, the upper levels of the postholes had a clayey fill and clay in the inner postholes had been baked when the inner circle had been burned down. This was proved by a thermoluminescent date contemporary with the circle. While no wattle impressions were found in this fired material, the clay is unlikely to be derived from the gravels themselves, but may well represent clay or daub washed off from wattle screens. Yet again the evidence is not conclusive but if care was taken to define proscribed entrances, then this scant evidence may well hint at obstructions in other potential yet unintended routes.

More evidence survives at a waterlogged timber circle at Bleasdale in Lancashire. This site comprises an outer palisade marked by a stockade of upright contiguous posts with stouter posts spaced intermittently round the perimeter. Inside this palisade and on a different orientation, was a small class I single entranced henge monument containing a

107   Stonehenge: the epitome of timber circles.

timber circle of well-spaced posts with a short avenue leading off to the east. There was a central grave containing Collared Urns. Only one narrow trench appears to have been excavated across the waterlogged ditch and here was found birch poles laid parallel to each other and interpreted as ditch flooring. While it is dangerous, in a ritual context, to look entirely for practical explanations for given observations, nevertheless, the flooring of a ditch in such a manner seems somewhat curious. Might these poles not represent the elements of a fence of horizontal poles supported by the more massive uprights of the circle and which, with the decay or dismantling of the monument, had collapsed or been pulled down into the ditch? Only further, more modern excavation might answer this question.

The reconstruction of timber circles is fraught with difficulty, speculation and personal preference. As they vary so considerably in their ground plans and geographical distribution, it may also be true that no one design should be envisaged but rather that timber circles represent the decayed and ravaged remains of a monument type as varied in its architecture as churches are today. Within the variety, however, there may be common threads of purpose and design. We may lament, with the stone circle authority with whom this chapter began, that by their nature timber circles no longer exist but this no longer appears to be the case. In Stonehenge they live on, fossilised and preserved. Stonehenge has no parallels or antecedents amongst the stone circle class, but in timber circles the architectural similarities are too close to ignore and by regarding Stonehenge as such, some, though by no means all, of its mysteries disappear (**fig 107**).

Gazetteer

Name	Arminghall, Norfolk
NGR	TG239060
Description	Horseshoe, open to the SW, of 8 large posts set in postholes each attended by a ramp facing to the south
Context	Within and earlier than a double-ditched henge monument
Dating	Henge with primary Beaker pottery acts as a *terminus ante quem*. Radiocarbon date of 4440±150 BP (BM-129)
Dimensions	13m diameter
References	Clark, 1936

Name	Balfarg, Fife
NGR	NO281032
Description	Multiple circle of at least 6 rings, badly eroded, with an entrance porch to the W. There also appears to be a southern orientation judging by the distribution of some finds, a causeway through the henge ditch and an apparent gap in the circles at this point
Context	Within a henge monument. Secondary Bronze Age burials. Replaced by a stone circle
Dating	Grooved Ware. Radiocarbon dates from the filling of the postholes 4315±60 BP (GU-1163), 4180±50 BP (GU-1160), 4035±50 BP (GU 1161), 4270±60 BP (GU-1162)
Dimensions	Ring A, 15 posts and 25m diameter. In all other circles the numbers of posts are uncertain. The diameters are as follows: Ring B — 47.6m, Ring C — 15m, Ring D — 41.7m, Ring E — 50m and Ring F — 71.4m
References	Mercer, 1981: Mercer *et al.* 1988

Name	Ballynahatty, Co. Down
NGR	J327677
Description	Double circle of huge post-pits surrounding a rectangular post setting. 33 posts in the outer circle and 25 in the inner. There is an entrance gap to the SE
Context	Set within a palisaded enclosure and within a henge complex
Dating	Grooved Ware
Dimensions	Inner circle 10m diameter, outer circle 15m diameter
References	Hartwell, 1994; 1998

Name	Barnack, Cambridgeshire
NGR	TF081066
Description	Regular single circle of 24/5 pits

Context   Approx 350m ESE of the Barnack cursus in an area of ring-ditch cropmarks

Dimensions Approximately 20m in diameter

References Simpson 1993

Name   Bleasdale, Lancashire

NGR   SD577460

Description Small single circle of 11 posts with an entrance porch to the E and with a central grave. Waterlogged wood from the surrounding ditch may suggest horizontals between the uprights

Context   Within a penannular ring-ditch, itself within a palisaded enclosure with an entrance to the NW

Dating   Collared Urn from the central grave. A radiocarbon date of 3760±90 BP (NPL-69) is unreliable since it is uncertain whether the wood came from the inner circle or outer palisade

Dimensions 11m diameter

References Varley, 1938: Council for British Archaeology, *Archaeological Site Index to Radiocarbon Dates for Great Britain and Ireland,* section 4B.1

Name   Bow, Devon

NGR   SS707016

Description Oval of 19 pits clearly visible as cropmarks within a class II henge

Context   Within henge

Dating   Context

Dimensions Approx 30m E-W by 18m N-S

References Griffith, 1985

Name   Brenig 44, Denbighshire

NGR   SH983572

Description Single circle of 20 posts, possibly with associated stakeholes including some central stakeholes

Context   Outside a ring cairn and below the external bank

Dating   Context

Dimensions 22.8m diameter

References Lynch, 1993

Name   Caebetin Hill, Powys

NGR   SO126865

Description An oval of 36 posts with larger posts in the E and W and a large edge-set stone immediately outside and due S of the circle. The oval itself is orientated N-S. There is an internal hearth and cremation deposit

Context   Below Bronze Age barrow

Dating   Context

Dimensions 6m N-S by 4.9m E-W

References   Jerman, 1932

Name   Caerloggas Barrow I, Cornwall
NGR   SX017565
Description An irregular circle of 43 posts, not all lying on the true circumference of
                 the circle, set around a central tor
Context   Below a later early Bronze Age ring-bank
Dating   Context
Dimensions   17m diameter
References   Miles, 1975

Name   Caerloggas Barrow III, Cornwall
NGR   SX017565
Description An irregular, slightly flattened circle of 8 posts set outside a ring-bank
Context   Associated with ring-bank
Dating   Context
Dimensions   25m diameter
References   Miles, 1975

Name   Cairnpapple Hill, West Lothian
NGR   NS987717
Description An oval of 24 posts with entrance to the SSE and a radial pairing in NNW
Context   Within a class II henge monument and later replaced by a stone circle
Dating   Context
Dimensions   31.5m by 27m
References   Piggott, 1947-8: Mercer, 1981: Barclay & Grove, 1998

Name   Charnham Lane, Hungerford, Berkshire
NGR   SU334692
Description Small circle of seven posts set around a central hearth and internal pits
Dating   Associated with Aldbourne cups of the early Bronze Age. A radiocarbon
                 date of 3360±40 BP (BM-2737) was recovered from pit 5008
Dimensions   6m in diameter
References   Ford, 1991

Name   Cocksbarrow, Cornwall
NGR   SW985563
Description An irregular double circle of 46 posts each, set around a central pit and
                 with an entrance to the SE
Context   Below a later early Bronze Age ring-cairn
Dating   Context
Dimensions   Outer circle is 20.9m diameter while the diameter of the inner circle is 20m
References   Miles, H. & T. J. 1971: Miles, 1975

Name   Coneybury Henge, Wiltshire
NGR   SU134416
Description   Possibly double circle, only partially excavated. Contains internal pits
Context   Set within a henge
Dating   Grooved Ware associations. Radiocarbon date of 4200±110 BP (OxA 1408), 4370±90 BP (OxA-1409)
Dimensions   Inner circle 3m diameter, outer circle 25m diameter
References   Richards, 1990

Name   Conygar Hill, Dorchester, Dorset
NGR   SY694891
Description   Small single circle of eight posts with slightly wider gaps to the NW and E
Context   Within segmented ring-ditch
Dating   Context
Dimensions   8m in diameter
References   Woodward & Smith, 1987

Name   Croft Moraig
NGR   NN797472
Description   Small single circle below a later stone circle. The timber phase has an entrance porch in the East, has outlying posts, and surrounds a central hearth and pit.
Context   Preceeds a stone circle
Dating   Context. There is also earlier Neolithic pottery from the site but this may be residual
Dimensions   Comprises 14 posts and has a diameter of 7.9m
References   Piggot & Simpson, 1971

Name   Deeping St Nicholas 28, Lincolnshire
NGR   TF174132
Description   Ring of posts set in a continuous trench as part of an embellishment around an existing early Bronze Age mound
Context   Part of a multi-phased barrow
Dating   Context
Dimensions   *c.*27m diameter
References   French, 1991

Name   Dorchester on Thames Site 3 (Oxfordshire)
NGR   SU587957
Description   An oval of 12 postholes containing the carbonised remains of 13 posts which had been burnt prior to the placing of cremations in the upper fills of the postholes. The SW posthole contained the remains of two posts in the same socket. There is a possible entranceway, marked by a wider gap between posts, in the NW
Context   Situated within the SE half of the Dorchester cursus

Dimensions   20m SE-NW x 17m
Dating   C14 dates of 4050±110 BP (BM-2161R), 4100±120 BP (BM-2162R) and 4120±120 BP (BM-2164R). Grooved Ware was also associated with the secondary cremations which act as a *terminus ante quem*
References   Bradley & Chambers, 1988: Whittle *et al.* 1992

Name   Dorchester-on-Thames, Site IV
NGR   SU569957
Description   Single penannular circle of 8 pits with entrance gap to the E. Re-interpreted as having held posts
Context   Within the cursus. Secondary use as a cremation cemetery
Dating   Context
Dimensions   8m diameter
References   Atkinson *et al.* 1951: Gibson, 1992: Whittle *et al.* 1992

Name   Dorchester-on-Thames, Site V
NGR   SU569957
Description   Single penannular circle of 14 pits with entrance gap to the W. Re-interpreted as having held posts. There appears to be evidence for the duplication of posts in one posthole
Context   Within the cursus. Secondary use as a cremation cemetery
Dating   Context
Dimensions   11.5m diameter
References   Atkinson *et al.* 1951: Gibson, 1992: Whittle *et al.* 1992

Name   Dorchester-on-Thames, Site VI
NGR   SU569958
Description   Single penannular circle of 12 pits with entrance gap to the W. Re-interpreted as having held posts. There appears to be evidence for the duplication of posts in one posthole
Context   Within the cursus. Secondary use as a cremation cemetery
Dating   Context
Dimensions   11.5m diameter
References   Atkinson *et al.* 1951: Gibson, 1992: Whittle *et al.* 1992

Name   Dorchester-on-Thames, Mount Farm, Berinsfield, Oxfordshire
NGR   SU583968
Description   Single circle of 14 posts with a larger entrance gap just E of N
Context   Within but eccentric to ring-ditch
Dating   Undated. Cuts early Neolithic pit
Dimensions   Oval 6.4m N-S by 5.6m E-W
References   Inf Alisdair Barclay, Oxford Archaeological Unit

Name   Durrington 68, Wiltshire
NGR   SU151433
Description A strange oval-sub-rectangular stakehole wall with two large entrance postholes in the SE and a second gap to the NE. The structure surrounds a rectangular setting of 4 large posts
Context   Covered by a round barrow and cut by the barrow ditch
Dating   Grooved Ware pottery from the postholes, including internally decorated bowls
Dimensions 14.6 by 10.1m
References Cunnington, 1929: Pollard, 1995

Name   Durrington Walls North Circle, Wiltshire
NGR   SU150438
Description A single circle of substantial posts later replaced by a double circle. It is approached by an avenue to the S. In phase 2 the avenue is to the SSW and is blocked by a screen arrangement
Context   Within a large henge monument
Dating   Grooved Ware associated with both phase 1 and 2, Radiocarbon date for phase 2 of 3905 ± 110 BP (NPL-240)
Dimensions Phase 1 diameter of 30m, phase 2 diameters are 14.4m for the outer circle consisting of 20 posts and 5m for the inner, consisting of 4 posts
References Wainwright & Longworth, 1971

Name   Durrington Walls South Circle, Wiltshire
NGR   SU150438
Description A multiple circle of four rings later replaced by a multiple circle of 6 rings. Phase 1 is attended by a screen to the SW while in phase 2 the entrance is marked by substantially larger posts. The site was not completely excavated
Context   Within a large henge monument
Dating   Grooved Ware associated with both phase 1 and 2. Radiocarbon date for phase 1 of 3760 ± 148 BP (NPL-239). Radiocarbon dates for phase 2 of 3950 ± 90 BP (BM-396), 3900 ± 90 BP (BM-395) and 3850 ± 90 BP (BM 397)
Dimensions Phase 1: Circle A, 30.04 diameter; Circle B, 23.25m diameter; Circle C, 14.75m diameter; Circle D, 2.25m diameter and consisting of 6 posts.
              Phase 2: Circle A, 38.9m diameter; Circle B, 35.72m diameter; Circle C, 29.35m diameter; Circle D, 22.9m diameter; Circle E, 15.2m diameter; Circle F, 10.75m diameter
References Wainwright & Longworth, 1971

Name   Etton (Etton Landscape Site 2), Cambridgeshire
NGR   TF135075
Description Aerial photographs of an irregular ring-ditch with internal pits, each containing a massive post and set in a broadly trapezoid setting

Context   Within a multi-phased henge complex
Dating   Ebbsfleet Ware provides an *terminus ante quem*
Dimensions   12.5m by 5m at its widest
References   Pryor, 1987

Name   Eynsham, Oxfordshire
NGR   SP425086
Description Possible site. A circle of 26 visible pits can be seen on the aerial photograph within the complex of the Eynsham barrow cemetery. There are hints of external pits
Context   Within a barrow cemetery
References   RCHME aerial photograph No. SP4208/127, frame No 2160/1090

Name   Ferrybridge N, West Yorkshire
NGR   SE476241
Description Single circle of 13 evenly spaced posts set around a single central post
Context   Within a henge complex
Dating   Context
Dimensions   16m diameter
References   Information from J. Hedges

Name   Ferrybridge S, West Yorkshire
NGR   SE476240
Description Single circle of 12 evenly spaced posts set around a single central post
Context   Within a henge complex
Dating   Context
Dimensions   16m diameter
References   Information from J. Hedges

Name   Flixton Park Quarry, Suffolk
NGR   TM 30288631
Description Single sub-circular enclosure with NW entrance. A small stakehole built rectangular structure is at its centre and there are other pits within and around it
Context   Cut by ring-ditch associated with Collared Urn
Dating   Associated with Grooved Ware
Dimensions   20m diameter
References   Boulter, 1997

Name   Forteviot, Perthshire
NGR   NO053169
Description Circle of pits visible on aerial photographs
Context   Within palisaded enclosure. Encircling hengiform monument
Dating   Context

Dimensions	Approx 40m diameter
References	Harding & Lee, 1987

Name	Goldington, Bedfordshire
NGR	TL079503
Description	Flattened circle of 14 cirumferentially paired posts with the pairing changing to radial in the pair opposite the SW entrance
Context	Within a penannular ring-ditch. Possibly secondary internal but acentric cremation deposit
Dating	Context within ring-ditch
Dimensions	15.5m diameter
References	Mustoe, 1988

Name	Gravelly Guy, Stanton Harcourt, Oxfordshire
NGR	SP40350535
Description	Penannular post circle open to the E. The spacing of the postholes varied from 1.6-2.6m. Postpipes and occasionally split timbers visible in some cases
Context	Within ring-ditch cemetery and general area of Prehistoric activity
Dating	Undated. Intrusive IA sherds in upper posthole fills. Pre-IA.
Dimensions	18.75m in diameter, 23 posts
References	Barclay *et al.* 1995

Name	Guiting Power Round Barrow 3, Gloucestershire
NGR	SP09562454
Description	Single circle of 65 posts with a slight inturned entrance to the SE. Evidence for trampling in the N half of the interior
Context	Below a round barrow
Dating	Associated with Beaker and Collared Urn sherds
Dimensions	13.4m diameter
References	Marshall, undated

Name	Hampton Lucy A, Warwickshire
NGR	SP251568
Description	Circle of pits within a ring-ditch visible on aerial photographs
Context	Within ring-ditch
Dating	Context
Dimensions	Approx 25-30m diameter
References	Information from John Hodgson, Warwickshire SMR

Name	Hampton Lucy B, Warwickshire
NGR	SP252567
Description	Circle of pits within a ring-ditch visible on aerial photographs
Context	Within ring-ditch

Dating   Context
Dimensions Approx 15-20m diameter
References Information from John Hodgson, Warwickshire SMR

Name   Haughey's Fort
NGR   H835453
Description A double circle of substantial post-pits set within an outer palisade within the interior of the fort
Context   Within later Bronze Age fort
Dating   2877±60 BP (UB-3386) from post-pit 267. 2824±37 BP (UB-3878) from posthole 112 in inner line of stockade. 2920±43 BP (UB-3879) from posthole 86 in inner line of stockade. 3591±147 BP (UB-3877) from central line of stockade
Dimensions 25m diameter
References Mallory, 1995

Name   Holme-next-the-sea
NGR   TF711452
Description Small circular site comprising a palisade perimeter of split oak posts. At the centre of the site was the upturned lower portion of an oak tree set in a deep pit. A forked post in the SW arc may have functioned as an entrance. The site is probably the remains of a palisade barrow.
Dating   Broad-bladed axe marks on the wood, radiocarbon dating and dendrochronology centre around 2000BC
Dimensions 6m diameter. Posts contiguous.
References Information from Mark Brennan, Norfolk Archaeological Unit.

Name   Holtby, E Yorkshire
NGR   SE66785426
Description Possible circle represented by a small single circle of close-set pits set within a ring-ditch cemetery
Dating   Context
Dimensions 12-14m diameter and consisting of 20-24 pits
References Information from D MacLeod (RCHME)

Name   Huntsmans Quarry, Naunton, Gloucestershire
NGR   SP12852570
Description Ring of ten evenly-spaced postholes set within a ring-ditch. Some smaller postholes at the entrance of the ring-ditch may be a porch structure. Eccentric cremation deposit
Context   Within penannular ring-ditch
Dating   Cord-impressed pottery, possibly Beaker or Food Vessel from the ring ditch
Dimensions 13.5m diameter. Posts set 4m apart
References Foster, 1994

Name	Kilmartin, Argyll
NGR	NS070950
Description	Circle approached by a timber avenue
Context	Cist burials, postholes pits and pit alignments in the vicinity. Appears to overlie the terminal of a pit-defined cursus. A smaller circle surrounding a pit lies to the S of the circle's interior
Dating	Presumed to be Neolithic in origin but used throughout the Bronze Age
Dimensions	46m diameter
References	Terry, 1998

Name	Knockaulin, Co Kildare
NGR	N820078
Description	Double circle of substantial posts set within a double palisaded enclosure with entrance to the NE. Central setting comprises a circle of posts with lines of posts radiating off
Context	Within Iron Age hillfort
Dimensions	Outer circle 25m diameter, inner circle 7m diameter. The double palisade has an overall diameter of some 44m
References	Lynn, 1991: Wailes, 1990

Name	Knowth, Co. Meath
NGR	N997734
Description	Circle of 21 postholes with an entrance to the E marked by a porch structure and with a rectangular setting of four posts within the monument
Context	Within a cemetery of satellite passage graves around the foot of the main Knowth mound. 12.5m to the E of the entrance to the E passage of the main mound
Dating	Grooved Ware. 4130±35 BP (GrA-445), 3985±35 BP (GrA-448)
Dimensions	8.5m diameter
References	Eogan & Roche, 1994; 1997

Name	Lawford, Essex
NGR	TM088308
Description	Single circular setting of posts with a black patch at the centre
Context	Within a ring-ditch
Dating	Associated with Grooved Ware
Dimensions	Approx 20m in diameter
References	Shennan *et al.* 1985

Name	Litton Cheney, Dorset
NGR	SY556917
Description	Small single oval with posts set in a bedding trench and interpreted as a hut by the excavator. There are internal postholes and pits

Context	Within a henge monument
Dating	Context
Dimensions	9m diameter, 32 posts
References	Catherall, 1976

Name	Loch Roag, Lewis
NGR	NB222325
Description	Antiquarian reference to an arc of charcoal-filled pits. These may possibly be postholes but the description is too vague
Context	Below the stone circle and cairn
Dating	Bronze age cairn provides a *terminus ante quem*
Dimensions	Approx 12.9m diameter
References	Stuart, 1857-60

Name	Longstone Field Circle 1, St Ishmaels, Pembroke
NGR	SM84870842
Description	Single circle of posts set within a bedding trench. Penannular stakehole setting within
Context	Situated within the area of a standing stone
Dating	Fragment of bronze from the packing material
Dimensions	6.5m diameter
References	Williams, 1989

Name	Longstone Field Circle 2, St Ishmaels, Pembroke
NGR	SM84870842
Description	Single circle of possibly 10 postholes resolved from a scatter of postholes to the S of circle 1
Context	Situated within the area of a standing stone
Dimensions	3.5m diameter
References	Williams, 1989

Name	Lugg, Co Dublin
NGR	O032246
Description	Multiple circular setting of three post rings and with an avenue to the N. Pairs of postholes are situated outside but concentric with the main circles and were interpreted as wooden 'trilithons'
Context	Inside henge-like monument later covered by a mound
Dating	LBA pottery provides *terminus ante quem*
Dimensions	Inner circle 16.75m diameter, middle circle 19.5m diameter and outer circle 21.3m diameter
References	Kilbride-Jones, 1950

Name	Machrie Moor I, Arran
NGR	NR912324

Description Double circle, the inner the larger, set around a horseshoe setting of five large posts open to the NW
Context Pits within the circle, later replaced by a stone circle.
Dating Associated with Grooved Ware. Radiocarbon dates of 4470±50 BP (GU 2316) and 3980±180 BP (GU-2325)
Dimensions Inner horseshoe, 5m diameter, inner circle, 14.5m diameter and the outer circle 19.5m diameter
References Haggarty, 1991

Name Machrie Moor XI, Arran
NGR NR912324
Description Single circle, with possible entrance gap (slightly wider space) to the N
Context Later replaced by a stone circle
Dating Stone circle acts as *terminus ante quem*
Dimensions 14.7m diameter
References Haggarty, 1991

Name Marden, Wiltshire
NGR SU090583
Description Single circle of posts with some internal postholes and pits
Context Within a henge monument
Dating Associated with Grooved Ware
Dimensions 10.5m diameter and consisting of 21 posts
References Wainwright *et al.*, 1971

Name Maxey pit circle A, Bardyke Field, Cambridgeshire
NGR TF125077
Description Ten oval pits set in circle. There were no traces of posts within the pits
Context Within the area of the outer ditch of a double-ditched henge. Cuts cursus ditch
Dating Sherd of possible Mildenhall pottery from Pit 4. Radiocarbon date of 1730±90 BP (GaK-657) is clearly too late and the sample was probably derived from later medieval material
Dimensions 14.2m diameter
References Simpson, 1985

Name Maxey pit circle B, Bardyke Field, Cambridgeshire
NGR TF125077
Description Ten oval pits set in circle. There were no traces of posts within the pits
Context Within the area of the outer ditch of a double-ditched henge
Dating Radiocarbon date of 1640±90 BP (GaK-658) from Pit 3 is clearly too late and the sample was probably derived from later medieval material
Dimensions 9.3m diameter
References Simpson, 1985

Name	Meldon Bridge, Peeblesshire
NGR	NT205404
Description	Small circle of abraded pits, possibly having held posts, surrounding a cremation deposit. Two pits in the NE appear to be duplicated. Possible entrance to the NNE
Dating	Context. Within the Neolithic palisaded enclosure
Dimensions	3m diameter, consisting of 12 pits
References	Burgess, 1976

Name	Meldon Bridge, Peeblesshire
NGR	NT205404
Description	Arc of pits representing a small circle of truncated postholes set around a central post. Each posthole had contained a post of 15-20cm in diameter
Dating	Context. Within the Neolithic palisaded enclosure
Dimensions	9m diameter, 7 pits excavated, others probably lay outside the excavated area
References	Burgess, 1976

Name	Meusydd B, Llanrhaeadr ym Mochnant, Powys
NGR	SJ13442522
Description	Cropmark B was discovered from the air by JK St Joseph in 1975 and comprises a small circle of 6 pits
Context	Within an area of ring-ditches
Dimensions	6m diameter
References	St Joseph, 1980

Name	Meusydd C, Llanrhaeadr ym Mochnant, Powys
NGR	SJ13462513
Description	Cropmark C was discovered from the air by JK St Joseph in 1975 and comprises a small circle of 10 pits
Context	Within an area of ring-ditches
Dimensions	10m diameter
References	St Joseph, 1980

Name	Milfield North, Northumberland
NGR	NT934348
Description	A single circle possibly with associated internal pits
Context	Below the presumed bank of a plough-truncated henge monument
Dating	Context
Dimensions	36.25m diameter
References	Harding, 1981

Name	Moel-y-Gaer, Denbighshire
NGR	SJ211691

Description   Seven posts set in a small circle within a hillfort and surrounding a large central pit, possibly a grave though the body had decayed and there were no grave goods

Context   Cut by Iron Age round house

Dating   Radiocarbon date of 3570±100 BP (HAR-1195)

Dimensions   7.4m diameter

References   Guilbert, 1973; 1975

Name   Moncrieffe, Tayside

NGR   NO132193

Description   Pit circle, possibly having originally held posts

Context   Within a henge monument and replaced by a stone circle

Dating   Context

Dimensions   6.5m diameter, consisting of 9 pits

References   Stewart, 1985

Name   Mount Farm, Berinsfield, Oxfordshire

NGR   SU583968

Description   Small circle of posts with apparent entrance gap to the NE

Context   Set a centrally within a ring-ditch

Dating   Early Neolithic pit acts as *terminus post quem*

Dimensions   6m diameter, 14 posts

References   Information from Alistair Barclay, Oxford Archaeological Unit

Name   Mount Pleasant, Dorset

NGR   SY710899

Description   Multiple circle of five rings with cardinally orientated aisles and with blocking stones within some aisles. Set around a rectangular central stone setting

Context   Within a ring-ditch within a large henge monument

Dating   Context. Radiocarbon date of 3630±60 BP (BM-668) from the stone structure. Other dates of 3988±84 BP (BM-667), 3941±72 BP (BM-666) and 3911±89 BP (BM-663) were obtained from the primary silts of the ditch surrounding the circles

Dimensions   Circle A: 38m diameter, consisting of 52 posts. Circle B: 30m diameter consisting of 48 posts. Circle C: 24.6m diameter, consisting of 36 posts. Circle D: 18.3m consisting of 24 posts. Circle E: 12.5m diameter, consisting of 24 posts

References   Wainwright, 1979

Name   Navan Site B, Armagh

NGR   H848451

Description   Circle of large post-pits set within a ring ditch

Context   Within the Navan enclosure

Dating	3140±90 BP (UB-974) from post-pit. 2628±50 BP (UB-188) from primary silts of the encircling ring ditch. 2615±75 BP (UB-979) from primary silts of the encircling ring ditch
References	Mallory, 1995

Name	Navan 40m structure, Armagh
NGR	H848451
Description	An outer wall, comprising double posts supported an outer wall of close set stakes and an inner 'skin' of planks. Within this wall were 4 concentric circles of posts set around one large upright set in a pit 2m deep. Aisles lead from the W up to and around this upright
Context	Site was covered by a cairn
Dating	Dendrochronological date for the central upright of 95/4 BC
References	Lynn, 1991; 1992

Name	Newgrange, Co Meath, Ireland
NGR	O007727
Description	Double timber circle only an arc of which was excavated. Possible entrance to the SE
Context	Within a passage grave complex and replacing a series of ritual pits
Dating	Beaker pottery plus radiocarbon dates of 4000±30 BP (GrN-12828) and 3930±35 BP (GrN-12829)
Dimensions	Inner circle 13m diameter, outer circle 19m diameter
References	Sweetman, 1987

Name	North Mains A, Tayside
NGR	NN928163
Description	Single circle with large postpits and attendant ramps all facing the outside of the circle. The circle appears to have been constructed in flattened segments
Context	Within but earlier than a henge monument. Food Vessel burials are secondary
Dating	Context. Radiocarbon dates of 4040±70 BP (GU-1354), 4105±60 (GU 1353), 4280±60 BP (GU-1352), 4015±65 BP (GU-1435) and 4130±60 BP (GU-1436) were also obtained
Dimensions	27m diameter and comprising 24 posts
References	Barclay, 1983

Name	North Mains B, Tayside
NGR	NN928163
Description	Single circle of small postpits
Context	Within and eccentric to circle A and the henge monument
Dating	Context
Dimensions	22.5m diameter and comprising 18 posts
References	Barclay, 1983

Name   Oakham, Burley Road, Leicestershire

NGR   SK867095

Description Three-phased, heavily plough-damaged circle. Phase 1 is a small oval of pits. Phase two is larger and on a different alignment with an entrance porch to the SE. Phase 3 comprises a small penannular setting

Dating   Neolithic pottery. Radiocarbon dates 3390±70 BP (OxA-2578) and 3565±80 BP (OxA-2421)

Dimensions Phase 1, incomplete, 20m diameter, 8 pits excavated. Phase 2, 34m x 22m, 23 pits. Phase 3, 10m x 7m, 7 pits

References Clay, undated; 1989: Hedges *et al.* 1992

Name   Oddendale, Cumbria

NGR   NY590137

Description Flattened double circle of 12 posts in each circle. Entrance gap to the SSW. Post ramps face outwards

Context   Below a ring cairn

Dating   Beaker acts as a *terminus ante quem*

Dimensions Outer circle 18m, inner circle 12m

References Turnbull, 1990

Name   Oelgragerrig, Gwynedd.

NGR   SH50558182

Description Penannular ring-ditch containing close-set but not contiguous timbers Entrance to the NW

Dimensions 4m diameter

References White, 1977

Name   Ogden Down Site 3 (Wiltshire)

NGR   ST971129

Description A double circle of posts with avenue of paired posts running off to the S and giving the site a cardinal orientation. The inner circle contains the larger posts and consists of 18 postholes and the outer circle consists of 34 posts

Context   Set around a ring ditch generally devoid of finds

Dimensions Inner circle has a diameter of 12.5m. The outer circle has a diameter of 15m

Dating   Oak charcoal from the inner post-ring 2870±50 BP (OxA-5125)

References Information from Martin Green

Name   Pont-ar-daf, Brecon, Powys

NGR   SN994200

Description Small circle of posts set within a bedding trench and surrounding a large flat stone

Context   Beneath a small cairn

Dating   3509±47 BP (UB-3216)

Dimensions 2.4m

References   Gibson, 1993

Name   Poole, Dorset
NGR   SZ057944
Description   A single circle with an avenue leading off to the SE through the causeway
                   of the enclosing penannular ring-ditch. There is a duplication of posts in
                   posthole 11 in the N and posthole 3 in the S
Context   Concentric with the inner edge of a penannular ring-ditch and the outer
                   edge of the mound of a bell-barrow. The primary burial had been robbed
Dating   3210±50 BP (GrN-1684) from charcoal from one of the posts
Dimensions   8m diameter, 19 posts
References   Case, 1952: Council for British Archaeology, *Archaeological Site Index to
                   Radiocarbon Dates for Great Britain and Ireland,* section 4B.3

Name   Radley, Barrow Hills I, Oxfordshire
NGR   SU518983
Description   Possible site. Semi-circle of 12 pits extending underneath a field boundary
Context   Within barrow cemetery
References   RCHME Film No.SU5198/46, Frame No. 4608/25
Name   Radley, Barrow Hills II, Oxfordshire
NGR   SU518983
Description   Possible site. Semi-circle of 12 pits extending underneath a field boundary
Context   Within barrow cemetery
References   RCHME Film No.SU5198/46, Frame No. 4608/25

Name   Raffin Fort, Co Meath
NGR   N202278
Description   Multi-ringed post setting comprising four or five circles of posts and
                   possibly set within a palisaded enclosure
Context   Within a Bronze Age and Iron Age palimpsest within the fort
Dating   2565±22 BP (laboratory number not quoted) acts as a *terminus ante quem*
Dimensions   9m diameter overall
References   Newman, 1995

Name   Rearsby, Leicestershire
NGR   SK6514
Description   Large circle of pits visible on aerial photographs. Appears to enclose an
                   oval ring-ditch
Dimensions   Approximately 50m diameter
References   Hartley, 1989

Name   The Sanctuary, Overton Hill, Wiltshire
NGR   SU118679
Description   Multiple circle of seven rings of posts. The innermost circle is eccentric to

the others and may be of a different period. The entrance posts are larger than the others and the West Kennet avenue leads off to the NE. Pollard has highlighted the increased deposition of material towards the rear (ie opposite the entrance) of the monument

Context   Replaced by a double stone circle

Dating   Associated with Grooved Ware

Dimensions   Outermost ring (A) 39.6m diameter, Ring B — 20.2m diameter, consisting of 34 posts, Ring C — 14.5m diameter consisting of 16 posts, Ring D — 10.5m diameter consisting of 12 posts, Ring E — 6.5m diameter consisting of 8 posts, Ring F — 4.2m diameter consisting of 8 posts, Ring G — 4m diameter consisting of 8 posts

References   Cunnington, 1931: Pollard, 1992

Name   Sarn-y-bryn-caled, Powys

NGR   SJ219049

Description Double circle with an entrance to the S marked by larger posts. Central secondary cremations associated with Barbed and tanged arrowheads (primary) and a Food Vessel (secondary)

Dating   Radiocarbon dates of 3730±40 BP (BM-2805) and 3670±40 BP (BM 2806) were obtained from the inner circle while dates of 3720±40 BP (BM-2808) and 3660±60 BP (BM-2807) were obtained from the outer circle

Dimensions   The inner circle measures 3m in diameter and consists of 6 posts while the outer circle measures 17.5m in diameter and consists of 20 posts

References   Gibson, 1994

Name   Shrewton 5d I, Wiltshire

NGR   SU088449

Description Double circle of stakes surrounding a central pit containing an unaccompanied cremation. The stake circles are not concentric and are approached by an irregular avenue, slightly curved and leading off for approximately 6m to the SSW. There are other apparently random and linear post arrangements within the area defined by the circles

Context   Below a bell barrow

Dating   Secondary Collared Urn burial provides a *terminus ante quem*

Dimensions   Outer circle approx 8m diameter, comprising 28 stakes. Inner circle approx 5m in diameter and comprising 31 stakes

References   Green & Rollo-Smith, 1984

Name   Springfield (Essex)

NGR   TL733072

Description A semi-circle of 13 postholes and truncated by a modern sewer trench. A series of internal pits may be associated with the circle to a greater or lesser degree

Context Situated within the NE terminal of the Springfield cursus
Dating Peterborough Ware associations
Dimensions 26.5m diameter
References Hedges & Buckley, 1981

Name Standlake 20, Oxfordshire
NGR SP383047
Description Single circle of posts lying outside a ring-ditch. One post in the WNW is duplicated
Dating Pottery from low in the ring-ditch was reported as being late Bronze Age but is now considered to be Deverel-Rimbury (inf. A. Barclay)
Dimensions 13.5m in diameter, consisting of 19 posts
References Catling, 1982

Name Stanton Drew, Somerset
NGR ST603630
Description Nine concentric circles of 1m diameter pits revealed by geophysical survey
Context Within a henge and replaced by a stone circle.
Dating Context
Dimensions Outer circle *c.*100m diameter.
References Information from Andrew David, English Heritage: David, 1988

Name Stonehenge I, Wiltshire
NGR SU123422
Description Single circle of posts (Aubrey holes) within the bank of the enclosure. The interpretation of the Aubrey holes is one of debate. Some cremation deposits in upper fills
Context Within a henge
Dating A radiocarbon date of 3798±275 BP (C-602) was obtained from charcoal from hole 32
Dimensions 86m diameter comprising 56 holes
References Atkinson, 1979: Cleal *et al.* 1995

Name Stonehenge II, Wiltshire
NGR SU123422
Description Multiple circle of posts within the central area of the enclosure. The circles are approached by an avenue from the S which is cut by a screen. The ground-plan is not totally discernable due to later rebuilding and comparatively recent excavation. It appears that at least 6 or 7 rings of posts may have been present
Context Within a henge. Later replaced by a stone version of a timber circle
Dating Context
Dimensions Approx 32m overall diameter
References Atkinson, 1979: Cleal *et al.* 1995

Name   Street House, Cleveland
NGR   NZ739189
Description   Single oval of posts set in a palisade trench with two pairs of opposed entrances. There was a central pit and 2-post structure
Context   Below a cairn
Dating   Radiocarbon dates of 3740±60 BP (BM-2566) and 3700±50 BP (BM 2567) were obtained from the palisade trench
Dimensions   9m diameter
References   Vyner, 1988

Name   Temple Wood, Argyll
NGR   NR826978
Description   Sockets below the stone circle were suggested to have originally held timber uprights. Internal pits and postholes were possibly associated with the timber phase
Context   Earlier than the stone circle on the same site
Dating   Radiocarbon date of 5025±190 BP (GU-1296) appears to be from old (oak) wood and is the earliest date from a timber circle
Dimensions   10.3m and comprising some possible 16 posts
References   Scott, 1988-9

Name   Upton Magna, Shropshire
NGR   SJ55521440
Description   Apparently spiral arrangement of pits visible on aerial photographs and approached by a single pit alignment. Unexcavated
Dimensions   Approximately 60m diameter and comprising 22 pits with a single post alignment 100m long, comprising 6 pits leading off to the NW
References   Cambridge University Committee for Aerial Photography photograph No.AVF23. D.N. Riley photograph No.506-26. Shropshire Sites & Monuments Record No.492

Name   Wasperton, Warwickshire
NGR   SP265585
Description   Single circle of close-set postholes, 1m apart, with a larger gap in the NE. There appears to be a duplication or replacements of posts immediately W of N and in the SE. The postholes sloped down from the N
Context   Within general area of BA and IA activity
Dimensions   6.5m in diameter, 17 posts (20 if duplicated/replaced posts are included)
References   Hughes & Crawford, 1995

Name   West Kennet (Palisade 2, Structure 1), Wiltshire
NGR   SU111682
Description   Palisade trench enclosing an irregular ring ditch
Context   Within palisaded enclosure

Dating   Grooved Ware
Dimensions 40m diameter
References Whittle, 1997

Name   West Kennet (Palisade 2, Structure 2), Wiltshire
NGR   SU111682
Description Palisade trench enclosing a circle of individual posts with rectangular porch-like structure to the S
Context   Within palisaded enclosure
Dating   Grooved Ware
Dimensions Surrounding palisade is approx 30m diameter. The timber circle measures approx 15m
References Whittle, 1997

Name   West Kennet (Palisade 2, Structure 3), Wiltshire
NGR   SU111682
Description Palisade trench enclosing a smaller palisade with a large, off-centre standing post
Context   Within palisaded enclosure
Dating   Grooved Ware
Dimensions Outer palisade 40-45m in diameter, inner ring approx 15m diameter
References Whittle, 1997

Name   Westfield I, Angus
NGR   NO629479
Description Cropmark circle of some 34 plus close-set pits set around a central 4-pit setting
Context   Same field as Westfield II
References RCAHMS, 1996

Name   Westfield II, Angus
NGR   NO629479
Description Cropmark circle of some 34 plus close-set pits set around a central 4-pit setting
Context   Same field as Westfield I
References RCAHMS, 1996

Name   Whitton Hill, Northumberland
NGR   NT933347
Description Single irregular post circle. The circle is flattened and some posts do not lie on the circumference. There are internal pits and postholes
Context   Within causewayed ring-ditch
Dating   Associated with Grooved Ware. A radiocarbon date of 3660±50 BP (BM 2266) was obtained from the central burial

Dimensions 6.5m diameter, 19 pits
References Miket, 1985

Name Withybushes, Rudbaxton, Pembrokeshire
NGR SJ250188
Description Single circle of approximately 30 pits visible on aerial photographs and arranged in a regular and apparently perfect circle
Dimensions Approx 20m diameter
References RCHAMW aerial photographs 905045-14-18; 925018-41-2

Name Woodhenge, Wiltshire
NGR SU150435
Description Large complex oval site comprising 6 ovals of posts. There are cardinal and solar orientations built within the monument which is set within but earlier than a henge. A child sacrifice was deposited in the centre of the monument
Context Precedes henge
Dating Associated with Grooved Ware. A Radiocarbon date of 3817±74 BP (BM-677) from the floor of the ditch and one of 3755±54 BP (BM-678) from the primary silts provide *termini ante quos* for the circle
Dimensions Circle A, 43.9m mean diameter and consisting of 60 posts. Circle B, 38.1m mean diameter and consisting of 34 posts. Circle C, 29.3m mean diameter and consisting of 16 posts. Circle D, 23.4m mean diameter and consisting of 19 posts. Circle E, 17.6m mean diameter and consisting of 18 posts. Circle F, 11.7m mean diameter and consisting of 12 posts
References Cunnington, 1929

Glossary

Association   Archaeologically, this term refers to artefacts which are unequivocally related to each other in time or space. For example, a number of artefacts which accompany a burial will be assumed to have been deposited at one time and are therefore associated. Artefacts from different contexts, however, are not associated, even though they may be contemporary. For example in a Peterborough Ware settlement, the potsherds from pits 1 and 2 may be broadly contemporary, but because they are from different contexts, they cannot be said to be associated.

Bedding trench   A trench dug to receive upright timbers. These trenches do not mean that the timbers were contiguous, but in some soils it is often easier to dig a trench rather than a series of postholes. They are often characterised by edge-set stones within the trench used for packing the uprights in position.

Causeway   Generally, in this work, the term is used to describe a break in a ditch. Thus the entrance of as henge would be by means of a causeway between the ditch terminals.

Excarnation   Some societies believe that, by removing the flesh and tissue from a skeleton, the journey from this life to the next is speeded up. Thus some bodies are defleshed either manually or by exposing the bodies to carrion birds and rodents. This process is known as excarnation — the deliberate (as opposed to natural) removal of flesh from a skeleton.

Geophysical survey   This term encompasses a number of different scientific techniques used to detect buried features. Most commonly used are resistivity meters which measure subtle changes in the resistance of the soil to an electrical charge or magnetometry which measures subtle changes in the magnetic properties of the soil. By analysing the differing results in both techniques, buried features can sometimes be detected.

Palisade   A substantial wooden fence composed of either contiguous or spaced uprights. These are generally massive walls, not unlike those timber uprights which form the walls of the cavalry forts of the American West.

Penannular   Almost a circle. Thus a circular ditched monument with an entrance causeway through the ditch would be described as penannular.

Radiocarbon dates   Radiocarbon dates, or rather radiocarbon determinations, are calculated by analysing the degree of decay of the radioactive carbon (Carbon 14) left in the organic material being studied. Each living organism takes in carbon from its food and surroundings and is constantly replenishing its carbon content. When the organism dies, this carbon intake ceases and the amount of radiocarbon decays. By analysing this rate of decay, a time since death can be estimated. This is conventionally released from a laboratory as a date BP with a margin of error thus: 4550±50 BP. BP means before present, conventionally placed at 1950. Thus the sample in this case was dated to 50 years either side of 4550 years before 1950 (or 2700-2500 BC). However, it has been realised for sometime that the rate of decay of radiocarbon is not as constant as originally believed and that some samples were considerably older than their radiocarbon dates. This was established using tree-ring dating and historical sources such as the Egyptian King Lists. Consequently all radiocarbon dates now have to be calibrated or corrected to calendar years using a computer programme such as the University of Oxford's *OxCal* or the University of Washington's *Calib*. All dates in this book have been calibrated using *OxCal*.

Stakeholes, postholes   These are pits of varying size which supported upright timbers. Postholes are usually larger and were dug out to receive a post and then refilled with packing material once the post was inserted. Stakeholes were usually formed when the wooden upright was driven into the ground. As a result, they often have tapered bases from the point of the stake.

Stratigraphy   The analysis of the relationship between and formation of various archaeological deposits and layers (strata) identified during excavation.

Terminus post/ante quem   This means 'date after/before which' and is used as a rough relative dating tool. If an archaeological feature, for example a ditch, has been dug through a Neolithic pit with, let's say, Peterborough pottery, then that pottery gives us a date after which the ditch was dug — ie the pottery acts as a *terminus post quem* since it was there before the ditch and therefore the ditch cannot be earlier. However, it does not give us the date of this ditch. It could be half an hour later or, on the other hand, several millennia later. *Terminus ante quem* acts in reverse. If our hypothetical Peterborough pit itself cuts an earlier feature, then that feature must be earlier and thus the Peterborough ware provides a *terminus ante quem*, a date before which the earlier feature was dug.

Bibliography

ApSimon, A.M., Musgrave, J. H., Sheldon, J., Tratman, E.K. & Wijngarden-Bakker, L. H. 1976. Gorsey Bigbury, Cheddar, Somerset. radiocarbon dating, human and animal bones, charcoals and archaeological re-assessment. *Proceedings of the University of Bristol Spelaeological Society*, 14 (2), 155-183.

Atkinson, R. J. C., 1979. *Stonehenge, Archaeology and Interpretation*. Revised edn. Harmondsworth: Penguin Press.

Atkinson, R.J.C., Piggott, C.M. & Sandars, N.K. 1951. *Excavations at Dorchester, Oxon*. Oxford: Department of Antiquities, Ashmolean Museum.

Barclay, A., Gray, M. & Lambrick, G., 1995. *Excavations at the Devil's Quoits Stanton Harcourt, Oxfordshire, 1972-3 and 1988.* Thames Valley Landscapes: The Windrush Valley, Volume 3, 88. Oxford: Oxford Archaeological Unit.

Barclay, G. 1983. Sites of the third millennium bc to the first millennium ad at North Mains, Strathallan, Perthshire. *Proceedings of the Society of Antiquaries of Scotland*, 113, 122-281.

Barclay, G. & Grove, D., 1988. *Cairnpapple Hill*, Edinburgh: Historic Scotland.

Becker, H. 1996. Kultplätze, Sonnentempel und Kalendarbauten aus dem 5. Jahrtausend v. Chr. — die mittelneolithischen Kreisanlagen in Niederbayern. In *Archäologische Prospektion: Luftbildarchäologie und Geophysik,* 101-122. Munich: Bayerisches Landesamt für Denkmalpflege.

Behrens, H. 1981. The first 'Woodhenge' in middle Europe. *Antiquity*, 55, 172-178.

Bénéteau, G., Cros, J.-P. & Gilbert, J.-M., 1992. L'enclos campaniforme/monolithe(s) des Terriers/Avrillé (Vendée). *Gallia Préhistoire*, 34, 259-288.

Boulter, S., 1997. *RMC Atlas Aggregates Ltd Quarry, Flixton Park, Flixton. Archaeological Excavation and Monitoring Archive Report (FLN 013)*. Report No. 97/53, Suffolk County Council Archaeological Service.

Bradley, R. & Chambers, R. 1988. A new study of the cursus complex at Dorchester on Thames. *Oxford Journal of Archaeology*, 7 (3), 271-89.

Britnell, W.J., Silvester, R.J., Gibson, A.M., Caseldine, A.E., Hunter, K.L., Johnson, S. Hamilton-Dyer, S. & Vince, A. 1997. A middle Bronze Age roundhouse at Glanfeinion, near Llandinam, Powys. *Proceedings of the Prehistoric Society*, 63, 179-198.

Burgess, C. B., 1976. Meldon Bridge: a Neolithic defended promontory complex near Peebles. In C.B. Burgess & R.F. Miket (eds), *Settlement and Economy in the Third and Second Millennia BC*, 151-179, BAR No. 33, Oxford: British Archaeological Reports.

Burl, H. A. W. 1976. *Stone Circles of the British Isles*. London & Newhaven: Yale.

Burl, H. A. W. 1983. *Prehistoric Astronomy*. Princes Risborough: Shire.

Burl, H.A.W. 1987. *The Stonehenge People*. London: J.M. Dent & Sons.

Burl, H.A.W. 1991. *Prehistoric Henges*. Princes Risborough: Shire.

Case, H.J. 1952. The excavation of two round barrows at Poole, Dorset. *Proceedings of the Prehistoric Society*, 18, 148-59.

Case, H.J. 1995. Beakers: loosening a stereotype. In I. Kinnes & G. Varndell (eds) *Unbaked Urns of Rudely Shape. Essays on British and Irish Pottery for Ian Longworth*, 55-68. Monograph 55, Oxford: Oxbow Books.

Catherall, P. D., 1976. Excavations at Litton Cheney, Dorset. In C.B. Burgess & R.F. Miket (eds), *Settlement and Economy in the Third and Second Millennia BC*, 81-100, BAR 33, Oxford: British Archaeological Reports.

Catling, H. W., 1982. Six ring-ditches at Standlake. In H. J. Case & A.W.R. Whittle (eds), *Settlement Patterns in the Oxford Region: Excavations at the Abingdon Causewayed Enclosure and Other Sites*. Research Report 44. London: Council for British Archaeology.

Clark, G. 1936. The timber monument at Arminghall and its affinities. *Proceedings of the Prehistoric Society*, 2, 1-51.

Clay, P., undated, *An Excavation at Burley Road, Oakham*. Interim report privately circulated.

Clay, P. 1989. Out of the unknown: approaches to prehistoric archaeology in Leicestershire. In A. M. Gibson (ed), *Midlands Prehistory*, 111-121. BAR 204. Oxford: British Archaeological Reports.

Cleal, R.M.J., Walker, K.E. & Montague, R. 1995. *Stonehenge in its Landscape. Twentieth Century Excavations.* Archaeological Report 10. London: English Heritage.

Cowie, T. G. 1988. *Magic Metal: Early Metalworkers in the North-east.* Aberdeen: University Anthropological Museum.

Cunnington, M.E. 1929. *Woodhenge. A Description of the Site as revealed by Excavations carried out there by Mr & Mrs B. H. Cunnington, 1926-7-8.* Devizes: George Simpson & Co.

Cunnington, M. E. 1931. "The Sanctuary" on Overton Hill near Avebury. *Wiltshire Archaeological and Natural History Magazine,* 45, 300-335.

Cunnington, R. H. 1931. "The Sanctuary" on Overton Hill. Was it roofed? *Wiltshire Archaeological and Natural History Magazine,* 45, 486-8.

David, A., 1988. Stanton Drew, *Past,* 28, 1-3.

Darvill, T. 1996. Neolithic buildings in England, Wales and the Isle of Man. In T. Darvill & J. Thomas (eds), *Neolithic Houses in Northwest Europe and Beyond,* 77-112. Monograph 57, Oxford: Oxbow Books.

Eogan, G. & Roche, H., 1994. A Grooved Ware wooden structure at Knowth, Boyne Valley, Ireland. *Antiquity,* 68, 322-30.

Eogan, G. & Roche, H. 1997. *Excavations at Knowth, 2.* Dublin: Royal Irish Academy & Department of Arts, Culture and the Gaeltacht.

Evans, J. G. 1984. Stonehenge — the environment in the late Neolithic and early Bronze Age and a Beaker age burial. *Wiltshire Archaeological and Natural History Magazine,* 78, 7-30.

Ford, S., 1991. An early Bronze Age pit circle from Charnham Lane, Hungerford, Berkshire. *Proceedings of the Prehistoric Society,* 57 (2), 179-81.

Foster, P. 1994. *Interim Report on the Excavations Carried out at Huntsman's Quarry, Naunton, Gloucestershire in 1994.* Privately circulated.

French, C. A. I., 1991. Excavation of Deeping St Nicholas Barrow Site 28, Lincolnshire. *Antiquity,* 65, 580-2.

Gibson, A. M. 1992. Possible timber circles at Dorchester-on-Thames. *Oxford Journal of Archaeology,* 11(1), 85-91.

Gibson, A. M. 1993. Excavations at Pont-ar-daf, Brecon Beacons, Powys — October 1989. *Bulletin of the Board of Celtic Studies,* 40, 173-189.

Gibson, A.M. 1994. Excavations at the Sarn-y-bryn-caled cursus complex, Welshpool, Powys and the timber circles of Great Britain and Ireland. *Proceedings of the Prehistoric Society*, 60, 143-223.

Gibson, A. M. 1998. Hindwell and the neolithic palisaded sites of Britain and Ireland. In A. Gibson & D. Simpson (eds) *Prehistoric Ritual and Religion: Essays in Honour of Aubrey Burl*, 68-79. Stroud: Sutton Publishing.

Gibson, A. M. & Woods, A. J. 1997. *Prehistoric Pottery for the Archaeologist*. 2nd edn. London: Leicester University Press.

Giffen, A.E. van 1930. *Die Bauart der Einzelgraber, I & II*. Leipzig: Mannus-Bibliothek.

Giffen, A. E. van 1938. Continental bell- or disc-barrows in Holland with special reference to Tumulus I at Rielsch Hoefke. *Proceedings of the Prehistoric Society*, 4, 258-71.

Glasbergen, W. 1954. *Barrow Excavations in the Eight Beatitudes: the Bronze Age Cemetery between Toterfout and Halve Mijl, North Brabant*. Groningen, and Jakarta: J. B. Wolters.

Green, C. & Rollo-Smith, S., 1984. The excavation of eighteen round barrows near Shrewton, Wiltshire. *Proceedings of the Prehistoric Society*, 50, 255-318.

Green, H. S. 1980. *The Flint Arrowheads of the British Isles*. BAR 75. Oxford: British Archaeological Reports.

Griffith, F. M., 1985. Some newly discovered ritual monuments in mid-Devon. *Proceedings of the Prehistoric Society*, 51, 310-315.

Guilbert, G., 1973. Moel-y-Gaer. *Archaeology in Wales,* 13, 23.

Guilbert, G., 1975. Moel-y-Gaer. *Archaeology in Wales,* 15, 33.

Haggarty, A. 1991. Machrie Moor, Arran: recent excavations at two stone circles. *Proceedings of the Society of Antiquaries of Scotland,* 121, 51-94.

Harding, A. F. 1981. Excavations in the prehistoric ritual complex near Milfield, Northumberland. *Proceedings of the Prehistoric Society*, 47, 87-135.

Harding, A. F. & Lee, G. E., 1987. *Henge monuments and related sites of Great Britain: Air photographic evidence and catalogue*. BAR 175, 1987. Oxford: British Archaeological Reports.

Hartley, F. 1989. Aerial Archaeology in Leicestershire. In A. M. Gibson (ed) *Midlands Prehistory*, 95-105. BAR 204. Oxford: British Archaeological Reports.

Hartwell, B. 1994. Late neolithic ceremonies. *Archaeology Ireland,* 8, 10-13.

Hartwell, B. 1988. The Ballynahatty complex. In A. Gibson & D. Simpson (eds), *Prehistoric Ritual and Religion*, 32-44. Stroud: Alan Sutton.

Hawley, W. 1928. Report on the excavations at Stonehenge during 1925 and 1926. *Antiquaries Journal*, 8, 149-76.

Hedges, J. D. & Buckley, D. G., 1981. *Springfield Cursus and the Cursus Problem*. Occasional Paper No.1, Essex County Council.

Hedges, R. E. M., Housley, R. A., Bronk, C. R. & van Klinken, G. J., 1992. Radiocarbon dates from the Oxford AMS system: Archaeometry datelist 14. *Archaeometry*, 34.1, 141-59.

Hristova, A., 1984, The flint material from Twisk, Province of North Holland. *Berichten van de Rijksdienst voor het Oudheidkundig Bodemonderzoek*, 34, 333-8.

Hughes, G. & Crawford, G., 1995. Excavations at Wasperton, Warwickshire, 1980-85. Introduction and Part 1: the Neolithic and Early Bronze Age. *Transactions of the Birmingham and Warwickshire Archaeological Society,* 99, 9-45.

Jerman, N., 1932. The excavation of a barrow on Caebetin Hill, Kerry, Montgomeryshire. *Montgomeryshire Collections,* 42 (2), 176-81.

Jong, J. de, 1998, Timber circles at Zwolle, Netherlands. In A. Gibson & D. Simpson (eds), *Prehistoric Ritual and Religion. Essays in Honour of Aubrey Burl*, 80-91. Stroud: Sutton Publishing.

Jong, J, de & Wevers, H. 1994. Cirkels en zonnenkalenders in Zwolle-Ittersumerbroek. *Archeologie en Bouwhistorie in Zwolle*, 2, 75-93,

Kilbride-Jones, H.E. 1950. The excavation of a composite early iron age monument with 'henge' fetures at Lugg, Co. Dublin. *Proceedings of the Royal Irish Academy*, 53C, 311-32.

Kinnes, I. 1992. *Non-megalithic Long Barrows and Allied Structures in the British Neolithic*. Occasional Paper 52. London: British Museum.

Lees, D. 1984. The Sanctuary: a neolithic calendar ? *Institute of Mathematics and its Applications,* 20, 109-114.

Lynch, F. M., 1993. *Excavations in the Brenig Valley: A Mesolithic and Bronze Age Landscape in North Wales*. Cambrian Archaeological Monograph 5. Cardiff: Cambrian Archaeological Association and Cadw: Welsh Historic Monuments.

Lynn, C. J., 1991. Knockaulin (Dun Ailinne) and Navan, some architectural comparisons. *Emania*, 8, 51-6.

Lynn, C. J. 1992. The Iron Age mound at Navan Fort: a physical realisation of Celtic religious beliefs ? *Emania*, 10, 25-32.

Mallory, J., 1995. Haughey's Fort and the Navan complex in the Late Bronze Age. In J. Waddell & E. Shee Twohig (eds), *Ireland in the Bronze Age, Proceedings of the Dublin Conference, April 1995*. Dublin: The Stationery Office.

Marshall, A. J., undated. Guiting Power 3 round barrow, Glos. summary of the site after completion of excavation. *Cotswold Archaeological Research Group Research Report No.9*.

Mercer, R. J. 1981. The excavation of a late neolithic henge-type enclosure at Balfarg, Markinch, Fife, Scotland, 1977-8. *Proceedings of the Society of Antiquaries of Scotland*, 111, 63-171.

Mercer, R. J. 1990. *Causewayed Enclosures*. Princes Risborough: Shire.

Mercer, R. J., Barclay, G. J., Jordan, D. & Russell-White, C.J., 1988. The neolithic henge-type enclosure at Balfarg — a re-assessment of the evidence for an incomplete ditch circuit. *Proceedings of the Society of Antiquaries of Scotland*, 118, 61-68.

Miket, R. 1985. Ritual enclosures at Whitton Hill, Northumberland. *Proceedings of the Prehistoric Society*, 51, 137-148.

Miles, H., 1975. Barrows on the St. Austell granite, Cornwall. *Cornish Archaeology*, 14, 5-82.

Miles, H. & T.J., 1971. Excavations on the Longstone Downs, St. Stephen-in-Brannel and St. Mewan. *Cornish Archaeology*, 10, 5-28.

Mustoe, R.S. 1988. Salvage excavation of a late neolithic and early bronze age ritual site at Goldington, Bedford. A preliminary report. *Bedfordshire Archaeology*, 18, 1-5.

Newman, C. 1995. Raffin Fort, Co. Meath: Neolithic and Bronze Age activity. In E. Grogan & C. Mount (eds), *Annus Archaeologiae. Proceedings of the DIA Winter Conference 1993*, 55-65.

Petrasch, J. 1990. Mittelneolithische Kreisgrabenanlagen in Mitteleuropa. *Bericht der Römisch-Germanischen Kommission*, 71, 407-564.

Piggott, S. 1940. Timber circles: a re-examination. *Archaeological Journal*, 96, 193-222.

Piggott, S., 1947-8. The excavations at Cairnpapple Hill, West Lothian, 1947-48. *Proceedings of the Society of Antiquaries of Scotland*, 10, 68-123.

Piggott, S. 1975. *The Druids*. London: Book Club Associates.

Piggot, S. & Simpson, D.D.A. 1971. Excavation of a stone circle at Croft Moraig, Perthshire, Scotland. *Proceedings of the Prehistoric Society*, 37, 1-15.

Pollard, J. 1992. The Sanctuary, Overton Hill, Wiltshire: A Re-examination. *Proceedings of the Prehistoric Society*, 58, 213-226.

Pollard, J. 1995. The Durrington 68 timber circle: a forgotten late Neolithic monument. *Wiltshire Archaeological and Natural History Magazine*, 88, 122-125.

Powell, T.G.E., Oldfield, F. & Corcoran, J.X.W.P. 1971. Excavations in zone VII peat at Storrs Moss, Lancashire, England, 1965-67. *Proceedings of the Prehistoric Society*, 37 (1), 112-37.

Pryor, F. 1987. An unusual new henge monument near Maxey and other happenings in the Peterborough Fenlands. *Fenland Research*, 4, 29-31.

RCAHMS, 1996. *Monuments on Record. Annual Review 1995-6,* 22. Edinburgh, RCAHMS.

Richards, C. & Thomas, J. 1984. Ritual activity and structured deposition in later neolithic Wessex. In R. Bradley & J. Gardiner (eds), *Neolithic Studies: A Review of Some Current Research*, 189-218, BAR 133. Oxford: British Archaeological Reports.

Richards, J. 1990. *The Stonehenge Environs Project*, Archaeological Report 16, London: English Heritage.

Ruggles, C., 1998. Ritual astronomy in the neolithic and beonze age British Isles: patterns of continuity and change. In A. Gibson & D. Simpson (eds), *Prehistoric Ritual and Religion: Essays in Honour of Aubrey Burl*, 203-208. Stoud: Alan Sutton.

Ruggles, C.L.N. & Whittle, A.W.R. (eds), 1981. *Astronomy and Society in Britain During the Period 4000-1500 BC*. BAR 88. Oxford: British Archaeological Reports.

St Joseph, J. K., 1980. Air reconnaissance: recent results 49. *Antiquity*, 54, 47-51.

Scott, J.G., 1988-9. The Stone Circles at Templewood, Kilmartin, Argyll. *Glasgow Archaeological Journal,* 15, 52-124.

Shennan, S. J., Healy, F. & Smith, I.F., 1985. The excavation of a ring-ditch at Tye Field, Lawford, Essex. *Archaeological Journal*, 142, 150-215.

Simpson, D. D. A. 1976. The later neolithic and Beaker settlement at Northon, Isle of Harris. In C. Burgess & R. Miket (eds), *Settlement and Economy in the Third and Second Millennia BC*, 221-232. BAR 33, Oxford: British Archaeological Reports.

Simpson, W. G., 1985. Exacavations at Maxey, Bardyke Field, 1962-3. In *The Fenland project, No.1: Archaeology and Environment in the Lower Welland Valley Volume 2*. By F. Pryor, C. French, D. Crowther, D. Gurney, G. Simpson and M. Taylor, 245-264. East Anglian Archaeology Report No.27.

Simpson, W.G., 1993. The excavation of Romano-British aisled buildings at Barnack, Cambridgeshire. *The Fenland Project No.7: Excavations in Peterborough and the Lower Welland Valley 1960-69*. East Anglian Archaeology 61, 102-126.

Stewart, M. E. C., 1985. The excavation of a henge, stone circle and metal-working area at Moncrieffe, Perthshire. *Proceedings of the Society of Antiquaries of Scotland*, 115, 125-50.

Stuart, J. 1957-60. Note of incised marks on one of a circle of standing stones in the Island of Lewis. *Proceedings of the Society of Antiquaries of Scotland*, 3, 212-4.

Sweetman, D. P. 1987. Excavation of a late neolithic/early bronze age site at Newgrange, Co Meath. *Proceedings of the Royal Irish Academy*, 87c, 283-98.

Terry, J. 1998. Upper Largie (Kilmartin Parish). *Discovery and Excavation in Scotland*, 1997, 19-21. Edinburgh: Council for Scottish Archaeology.

Turnbull, P., 1990. *Excavations at Oddendale, 1990, Interim Report*. Cumbria County Council Planning Dept.

Varley, W.J. 1938. The Bleasdale Circle. *Antiquaries Journal*, 18, 154-71.

Vayson de Pradenne, A. 1937. The use of wood in megalithic structures. *Antiquity*, 11, 87-92.

Vyner, B., 1988. The Street House Wossit: The excavation of a late neolithic and early bronze age palisaded ritual monument at Street House, Loftus, Cleveland. *Proceedings of the Prehistoric Society*, 54, 173-202.

Wailes, B., 1990. Dun Ailinne: a summary excavation report. *Emania*, 7, 10-21.

Wainwright, G. J., 1979. *Mount Pleasant, Dorset: Excavations 1970-71*. Research Report No.37. London: Society of Antiquaries.

Wainwright, G. J., Evans, J. G. & Longworth, I. H., 1971. The excavation of a late neolithic enclosure at Marden, Wiltshire. *Antiquaries Journal*, 51, 177-239.

Wainwright, G.J. & Longworth, I.H. 1971. *Durrington Walls Excavations: 1966-68.* Research Report No.29. London: Society of Antiquaries.

Warren, S.H., Piggott, S., Clark, J.G.D., Burkitt, M.C., Godwin, H & M.E. 1936. Archaeology of the submerged land surface of the Essex coast. *Proceedings of the Prehistoric Society*, 2, 178-210.

Waterbolk, H.T. & van Zeist, W. 1961. A bronze age sanctuary in the raised bog at Bargeroosterveld (Dr.). *Helinium*, 1, 5-19.

White, R. B., 1977. Rhosgoch to Stanlow Shell Oil Pipeline. *Bulletin of the Board of Celtic Studies*, 27, 463-490.

Whittle, A. W. R. , 1997. *Sacred Mound Holy Rings. Silbury Hill and the West Kennet palisade enclosures: a later Neolithic complex in north Wiltshire*, Monograph 74. Oxford: Oxbow Books.

Whittle, A. W. R., Atkinson, R. J. C., Chambers, R. & Thomas, N. 1992. Excavations in the neolithic and bronze age complex at Dorchester on Thames, Oxfordshire, 1947-52 and 1981. *Proceedings of the Prehistoric Society*, 58, 143-201.

Williams, G., 1989. Excavations in Longstone Field, St Ishmaels, Pembrokeshire. *Archaeologia Cambrensis*, 138, 20-45.

Woodward, P. J. & Smith, R. J. C., 1987. Survey and excavation along the route of the southern Dorchester by-pass, 1986-1987 — an interim report. *Proceedings of the Dorset Natural History and Archaeological Society*, 109, 79-89.

Index